THE FACILITATOR'S BOOK OF QUESTIONS

Tools for Looking Together at Student and Teacher Work

THE FACILITATOR'S BOOK OF QUESTIONS

Tools for Looking Together
at Student and Teacher Work

David Allen
Tina Blythe

Foreword by Gene Thompson-Grove

Teachers College,
Columbia University
New York and London

National Staff
Development Council
Oxford, Ohio

Published simultaneously by Teachers College Press, 1234 Amsterdam Avenue, New York, NY 10027 and by the National Staff Development Council, P. O. Box 240, Oxford, OH 45056

Library of Congress Cataloging-in-Publication Data

Allen, David, 1961–
   The facilitator's book of questions : tools for looking together at student and teacher work / by David Allen, Tina Blythe ; foreword by Gene Thompson-Grove.
      p. cm.
   Includes bibliographical references.
   ISBN 0-8077-4468-9 (pbk : alk. paper)
      1. School management and organization.   2. Group facilitation.   3. Teachers—Professional relationships.   I. Blythe, Tina, 1964–   III. Title.
   LB2806 .A525 2004
   371.102—dc22   20033068686

ISBN 0-8077-4468-9 (paper)

Printed on acid-free paper
Manufactured in the United States of America

10   09   08   07   06   3   4   5   6   7   8

For our parents,
James and Virginia Allen
Edker and Lorraine Blythe

Contents

Chapter 8
What Are the Challenges of Facilitating Protocols?   **100**

Chapter 9
How Do Facilitators Get Better?   **117**

Foreword

I love to facilitate—be it a protocol-guided conversation or some other kind of meeting or session—and I appreciate the work of really skilled facilitators when I am a participant in a group. However, I admit to being a bit skeptical of the value of books on facilitation, since most seem to focus on new sets of techniques, tricks, or recipes. *The Facilitator's Book of Questions: Tools for Looking Together at Student and Teacher Work* is a much-needed departure from that approach to facilitation—and should be useful to experienced and beginning facilitators alike.

What makes this book so different and so useful? First, it avoids a generic discussion of facilitation and instead places facilitation in a particular context, that of facilitating protocol-guided conversations about students' work and teachers' work. In doing this, the authors are able to ask facilitators to consider their own assumptions and beliefs—about their role as facilitators, about the purpose of the work they are facilitating, and about the group with whom they are working. Second, it avoids giving pat answers for potentially complex situations, and instead invites readers to consider the consequences—intentional or not—of the various "moves" they make as facilitators.

Finally, the book addresses the important question of facilitator stance, or disposition, challenging those of us who facilitate to ask ourselves: How am I reading this group, and how do I know I am right? What should I do, and how do I decide this is the best course of action? Do I really believe these people have the capacity to do the learning they say they want to do—and if I do, how do I best serve them and their learning? Certainly, in reading this book, facilitators will expand their repertoire and walk away with ideas and tips for responding to the wide range of facilitation issues that invariably come up in protocols. More important, however, the reader will be pushed to think about her

stance as a facilitator, as all of the ideas about *how* to respond are linked
to discussions of *why* one might want to respond in that way.

Facilitating protocols can be a tricky proposition. The task requires
the facilitator not only to "show up," but to be fully present and completely attentive to the group and its learning. The protocols can help,
acting, as the authors say, as a kind of co-facilitator. Protocols help
build equity into the conversation; they help group members build new
skills and habits; they help make efficient use of time; and they help
build a useful agenda for almost any kind of meeting. However, they
don't stand on their own, and they require a firm yet gentle hand on the
part of the facilitator. A skillfully facilitated protocol not only creates
the possibility of a group doing new, significant learning together—
learning that ultimately will benefit students—but also can help a
group build the kind of trust that allows it to tackle the really important questions about teaching and learning. Addressing such questions
requires individuals' willingness to share and, often, reconsider their
own privately held beliefs.

I think about this kind of facilitation as being full of tensions—tensions that as a facilitator I want to, in the spirit of this book, manage
rather than resolve. I want to be an advocate for the presenter's success,
yet also be in service to the whole group and its learning. I want to facilitate with a light hand, yet be firm in helping the group stick to the
agreements it has made about how group participants will talk together. I want to honor the steps and intention of the protocol, yet not feel
by the end of the session as if the protocol somehow has used us. I
know the protocol will demand a certain rhythm by its very structure,
yet I want to tap into the natural rhythm of the group. I want to be an
active facilitator—one that group members can count on to keep the
process safe so they can have potentially risky conversations with each
other. Yet I know that sometimes the best thing I can do or say as the
facilitator is nothing, because sometimes it has to be uncomfortable in
order for group members to learn and grow. I want to be a fully con-
tributing member of the group, yet I know that good facilitation sometimes demands that I give my full attention to focusing on the process
of the conversation.

I remember the day I turned the corner in my thinking about myself
as a facilitator. The conversation that day had been challenging, and the

group confronted some deeply held beliefs about expectations for students. I knew that individuals in the group had moved to a new, more productive place in their thinking. As I read the reflections written by group members about the session, I was struck by how all of them talked about their learning, about their students, about their practice, and about how other group members had challenged them to see the student work and their assumptions differently. There was not one mention about the role I had played as facilitator. That is when I understood what is for me now the most important maxim about facilitating protocol conversations: "This is not about me." Facilitators with a broad repertoire of responses and sophisticated ways of thinking about their craft are critical to the collaborative work of teachers. But, in the end, the work is not about the facilitator, or the facilitation, or the protocol. It is, first and foremost, about the learning the presenter and the group do together on behalf of students.

—GENE THOMPSON-GROVE

Acknowledgments

Many people facilitated the writing of this book . . .

The authors thank the following colleagues who have collaborated with us and, in a variety of ways, shared with us their wisdom about and skill in facilitation: Carin Aquiline, Daniel Baron, Phyllis Brethholz, Linda Clark, Beth Delforge, Alan Dichter, Corina Haley, Constanza Hazelwood, Frances Hensley, Frank Honts, Katy Kelly, Joe McDonald, Nancy Mohr, Monica Osborn, Barbara Powell, Steve Seidel, Debra Smith, Gene Thompson-Grove, and Diana Watson.

We also have had the privilege of working on issues of facilitation with teachers and administrators at a number of schools, school districts, conferences, and institutes. In particular, we thank

- Chelmsford School District in Chelmsford, MA (especially Karen Mazza)
- Fisher Hill Elementary School in Orange, MA (especially Sheryl Brault and Moira O'Brien)
- The Harbor School in Boston, MA (especially Mark Clarke, Karen Engel, Scott Hartl, Christina Patterson, and Joseph Zaremba)
- Jacob Hiatt Magnet School in Worcester, MA (especially Tony Caputo, Beth Creamer, and Mary Labuski)
- Lee County School District in Fort Myers, FL (especially Lynn Edward and Vicki Stockman)
- Forestdale Elementary School in Malden, MA (especially Maurine Chirichetti and Elaine McCarthy)
- Marblehead High School in Marblehead, MA (especially Beth Delforge and Marilyn Horwitz)
- New Canaan School District in New Canaan, CT (especially Donna Arrow)

- New York State Academy for Teaching and Learning in Albany, NY (especially Anne Schiano)
- Traverse City School District in Traverse City, MI (especially Dan Fouch, Lynn Katsaros, and Jane Mohr)
- Participants and facilitators at the Coalition of Essential Schools Fall Forum preconference session on looking at student work, November 2002
- Participants in the facilitation minicourses at the Project Zero Summer Institutes, 2002 and 2003
- Participants in Looking at Student Work: A Project Zero Workshop, April 2003
- Colleagues from the Looking at Student Work Collaborative (especially John Simmons)
- Colleagues from the Evidence Project, Project Zero—including Steve Seidel, Shirley Veenema, Denise Simon, Terri Turner, Linda Clark, Sarah Hendren, and Patricia Leon

Our thanks to Steve Seidel, Barbara Powell, and Gene Thompson-Grove for their thoughtful feedback on the manuscript, and to Brian Ellerbeck, our editor at Teachers College Press, for his encouragement.

Finally, we are particularly grateful to the National School Reform Faculty—especially Gene Thompson-Grove, Faith Dunne, Simone Waite, and Edorah Fraser—for allowing us to incorporate in this book selections from the excellent materials they have developed on facilitation and protocols.

THE FACILITATOR'S BOOK OF QUESTIONS

Tools for Looking Together
at Student and Teacher Work

Introduction

Most of us know the sheer pleasure of watching a basketball team or listening to a jazz band that is really working well together. Both situations involve a dynamic mix of roles, exchanges of information (not to mention of the ball), a balance between rules and structures (chords and set plays), and more improvised, opportunistic—even inspired— play. And often one player—perhaps the bandleader or the point guard (but possibly a hardworking forward or deft bassist)—performs in a way that makes the work of the others look and sound better. In short, a satisfying and effective collaboration unfolds before our eyes and ears.

While teachers' collaborative work is almost never as public as a jazz band's is or competitive in the way a basketball team's is, the idea of collaboration is increasingly central to the work of schools, for the adults in the building as well as the students. In a field notorious for the isolation of its practitioners, collegial collaboration within schools has made some great strides in recent years—although few would deny there is room for much more progress.

At the heart of most teacher collaboration is a conversation, or better, an ongoing series of conversations. Of course, conversations among teachers are not unusual. Think of the faculty room or staff meetings. But the conversations we focus on in this book are different. Unlike either informal faculty room conversations that tend to move naturally and quickly from topic to topic, or typical staff meetings that serve mainly to transmit information (begging the question, "Couldn't we have got that in a memo or e-mail?"), the conversations discussed in this book are opportunities for colleagues to reflect together on key questions about their practice and their students' learning (Ball & Cohen, 1999; Lieberman & Miller, 2000; Louis, Kruse, & Marks, 1996).

These conversations may happen within established groups such as a department or a grade-level team; however, they just as often take place within groups that assemble specifically to engage in exploration of or inquiry into the mysteries of teaching and learning. These groups go by different names, including

- critical friends groups
- collaborative inquiry groups
- study groups
- action research groups
- "looking at student work" groups

While the names suggest some distinctive features, these groups also share some important qualities (in addition to collaboration itself):

- A grounding in the actual work that students and teachers carry out in classrooms and schools
- A recognition that all participants in the group bring expertise as well as unique experiences and perspectives
- A focus (or set of foci) determined by the group and of deep significance to the group's members
- A commitment that group members make both to their own learning and to the learning of the group as a whole

Such groups often have two other features in common: A facilitator who helps to guide the group's work; and the use of "protocols"—that is, structures—that support the focused examination and discussion of students' and/or teachers' work.

The leader of a jazz group or the point guard on a basketball team looks for ways to use the structures and constraints of the melody or the game to provoke and support the efforts of individuals and the whole group or team. For facilitators of collegial conversations, protocols provide that set of structures and constraints. In this book, we focus on the parts facilitators play so that others in the group may play (and learn) better. The remainder of this brief introduction consists of just seven questions (leaving plenty for the rest of the book).

WHY A BOOK OF QUESTIONS FOR FACILITATORS?

As educators, we share an appreciation for the importance of asking and answering questions. Yehudi Menuhin, the brilliant violinist, recounted that his father asked him every evening not what he learned in school, but, "What questions did you ask in school?" The role of questions is as crucial in supporting adult learning as it is in supporting students' learning. Questions are the facilitator's most important tool—really a whole set of tools, since they take many forms, with different questions appropriate for different points in protocol-guided conversations (as well as before and after them). In some protocols, questions of different kinds are built into the structure of the protocol. But many of the questions that support participants' learning are asked by facilitators spontaneously in response to the group's conversation as it develops.

WHY A BOOK OF QUESTIONS FOR FACILITATORS OF *PROTOCOLS*?

Protocols, particularly those that serve to structure conversations about student and teacher work, have gained enormous popularity in recent years. Much existing wisdom about facilitating effective meetings is applicable in facilitating protocols. Yet protocol-guided conversations have particular features that distinguish them from other kinds of meetings or professional development sessions. These distinctive features—as well as the unique challenges that emerge in conversations using protocols—call for particular kinds of facilitation. Chapter 1 provides an overview of protocols, including three commonly used protocols for looking at student work and teacher work.

WHAT DO WE MEAN BY *STUDENT WORK* AND *TEACHER WORK*?

Many kinds of data are available for analyzing, assessing, and improving curriculum and instruction to support student learning and understanding: classroom grades and test scores, standardized test scores, research studies on particular curricula or instructional strategies, and so on. All offer important opportunities for educators' learning. In this book, we focus on just two kinds of data: (1) samples of work students produce or create in the classroom (usually), most commonly in response to an assignment or a task provided by their teacher, and (2) samples of the work teachers do to support students in their learning.

These samples often take physical form: student writing, problem solving, or visual products, as well as teachers' assignments, writing prompts, scoring criteria, rubrics, and so on. The tangible form of such data makes them ideal focal points for a protocol-guided conversation. Sometimes the work is presented in narrative form, such as a teaching "dilemma" (Cuban, 2001) or "critical incident" (Tripp, 1993), often supplemented or illustrated by physical "artifacts" like those mentioned above.

The forms of student and teacher work are nearly limitless. While we offer guidance to facilitators and presenting teachers on how to select samples to address different kinds of questions, the purpose of this book is not to identify better or worse student or teacher work to present, but to help educators more profitably learn from the everyday currency of classroom teaching and learning.

The relationship between teachers' work and students' work is critical and not yet well understood. Recent studies have begun to address the influence of teachers' assignments on students' capacity to produce work that demonstrates greater understanding or in-depth learning (Newmann, Lopez, & Bryk, 1998). Protocols offer one vehicle for teachers to explore for themselves how their own work affects student learning.

WHO IS THIS BOOK FOR?

In this book, we write about the facilitator without reference to how that facilitator was chosen, what her background is, what she does when she's not facilitating, and so on. The developmental path for facilitators is not well defined (although maybe it should be), and very few people facilitate groups as their primary job. Some facilitators are "insiders," typically teachers or administrators who take on the responsibility of facilitating groups of peers. These are typically lead teachers or mentor teachers for whom facilitation is one aspect of their teacher leadership. Other facilitators come from outside the school, for example, a school coach from the district, a partner organization, or a local university. Facilitating protocols is often just one aspect of the coaching they provide.

Insider and outsider facilitators can both play extremely valuable roles in supporting collaboration and learning in the school—indeed, in our view and others' (Moffett, 2000), having a combination of insider and outsider facilitators is optimal. Each brings different advantages and faces different challenges. Insiders know the school context and the people well. Because they are part of the day-to-day routine of the school, they can monitor the work's progress closely and tailor the work to fit the needs of the school. And, of course, they have a vested interest in its success. On the other hand, it can be challenging for teachers, especially, to take on a leadership role among their peers. They also may have had limited opportunities to develop the skills that contribute to effective facilitation.

Outsiders may not have as much difficulty taking on a unique role within the group: As outsiders, their status is somewhat unique to begin with. They often bring well-practiced skills and a range of experiences from facilitating in other school settings. However, removed from the day-to-day operations of the school, they are not in a good position to keep the work alive and growing in a sustained way. That kind of work depends on the commitment and efforts of the insiders, particularly school leaders and group members.

Despite these differences, we have found that a facilitator's skills, the questions she asks, and the actions she takes to guide a conversation do not vary dramatically depending on whether the facilitator is an insider or an outsider. In writing this book, we are drawing not only on our own facilitation experiences but also on the experiences and reflections of a range of facilitators with whom we have worked, insiders and outsiders, novice and experienced.

HOW IS THIS BOOK ORGANIZED?

Because the book focuses on facilitating protocols for looking at student and teacher work (including teacher dilemmas), we begin in Chapter 1 with an in-depth look at protocols and how they support conversations about critical issues of teaching and learning. Facilitators, as well as the groups they work with, need to understand the commonalities among protocols, as well as key differences in their purposes and structures. Of course, with so many varied protocols in current use, there is much more to say about protocols than we can say here; the chapter provides references to other resources with more extensive treatments of particular protocols.

In Chapter 2, we discuss how protocol-guided conversations are different from other kinds of professional or staff development (e.g., workshops, trainings, courses, coaching relationships, and so on). Understanding these differences is crucial to understanding how the facilitator's role is different from that of presenters, instructors, mentors, and others who lead more familiar kinds of professional development sessions. Just as professional collaboration challenges norms of teacher isolation in schools, facilitation (as we define it) challenges the norms of staff development as it usually has been practiced.

Chapter 3 offers an overview of the facilitator's role. In it we describe the three large spheres of responsibility to which facilitators need to attend: the learning of the group, the logistics of the meetings, and the longevity of the work within the school. In carrying out these responsibilities, facilitators are aided by three broad sets of abilities (or "thinking dispositions"): the ability to "read" the group, the ability to respond to its needs, and the ability to reflect on and learn from their own efforts and the work of the group—and to encourage the reflection of other participants.

Chapter 4 provides a more specific view of a facilitator's work, focusing on the things facilitators do and say in the course of a conversation using a protocol. Some of these "moves" are predictable and employed frequently; others emerge in response to very specific situations. We group these moves into three categories: getting the (protocol-guided) conversation started, moving through the conversation, and debriefing the conversation.

Protocols involve participants in asking and exploring different categories of questions. Chapter 5 provides a closer look at the differences among the three kinds of questions most commonly invited by protocols: focusing questions, clarifying questions, and probing questions.

In Chapter 6, we step back from the protocol-guided conversation to look at what facilitators do to prepare for it. This preparation involves taking care of the logistics, an important component of the work. It also requires working with the presenter to help clarify her goals for sharing her students' work (or her own) and to help her understand her role in the conversation. We also consider some of the ways facilitators work with presenters and other participants after the protocol ends to encourage continued reflection and plan for future conversations.

Chapter 7 treats a more specific and complex aspect of the facilitator's work: critical decisions about choosing which protocol to use, modifying a protocol while the conversation is underway, adapting existing protocols, and developing new protocols.

Chapter 8 presents a sampling of the challenges that crop up in protocol-guided conversations. The list of challenges is not definitive (new ones come up all the time), and none of these challenges has a foolproof solution. Instead of offering our responses to the challenges (which would be just that—ours, and not the only or the best ones), we suggest a range of moves facilitators might make in response to each challenge.

In reading these chapters—and mentally adding up all of the things facilitators do—the reader may think that facilitation is a daunting task. It is! But so is teaching a good lesson or being a good administrator. The best facilitators recognize that the role is demanding and challenging. They enjoy the problem solving required to meet those challenges. And they are willing to learn through experience, through reflecting on how they facilitate, and through talking to others who do it—as well as to participants in the groups they facilitate. In Chapter 9, we consider how facilitators get better at supporting the learning of groups through observation, emulation, experimentation, feedback, and reflection.

WHAT *DOESN'T* THIS BOOK DO?

This book is about facilitating conversations using protocols. It does not provide a detailed description of various protocols, their theoretical underpinnings, and their uses. For this kind of examination, see especially *The Power of Protocols: An Educator's Guide to Better Practice* (McDonald, Mohr, Dichter, & McDonald, 2003) and *Assessing Student Learning: From Grading to Understanding* (Allen, 1998).

Good facilitation is one of the conditions for using protocols effectively as tools for exploring issues of teaching and learning. Other conditions need attention, too: How will groups be composed? How is time made available for groups to meet? How is the groups' work aligned with relevant school goals? And so on. These conditions are discussed in depth in other resources, such as *Teaching as Inquiry: Asking Hard Questions to Improve Practice and Student Achievement* (Weinbaum, Allen, Blythe, Simon, Seidel, & Rubin, 2004) and *The Evidence Process: A Collaborative Approach to Understanding and Improving Teaching and Learning* (Evidence Project Staff, 2001).

HOW MIGHT THIS BOOK BE USED?

Learning about facilitating protocols, like teaching (or playing basketball or jazz), doesn't lend itself to a step-by-step approach. Rather than attempting to impose a sequence of facilitation actions, the book is organized topically. It is intended to provide plenty of room for an exploration of the complex, occasionally frustrating, and frequently satisfying role of facilitator.

This exploration may be profitably undertaken alone, reading and reflecting on the chapters in an order that makes sense to the individual. The reader won't be surprised to learn, however, in a book devoted to collaborative learning, that we believe the book gains power as a resource when it is a starting point for discussion and reflection among those who facilitate or participate in groups focused on teaching practice and student learning.

The appendices at the end of the book provide further resources for facilitators, including some specific activities that can be used by groups to develop their skill in using protocols. While these activities provide an obvious opportunity for collaborative conversation with colleagues, we feel that even the more descriptive sections of this book should be the launching points for discussion, interpretation, disagreement, and adaptation.

This is, finally, the reason we settled on *The Facilitator's Book of Questions* as the title and organizing principle for the book: Ultimately, there are no easy solutions to any important challenges of facilitation. The questions in this book are meant to be asked, teased apart, and considered from various perspectives. We hope they will lead to a rich discussion among practicing, developing, and potential facilitators . . . as well as to new questions that never occurred to the authors.

Chapter 1

What Are Protocols and How Do They Work?

Sometimes, powerful opportunities to learn with and from others occur spontaneously and naturally in the course of daily life. A casual lunchtime conversation about what to make for dinner unexpectedly turns into a thoughtful exchange about the relationship between food and culture. Discovering a common interest (woodworking, travel, nineteenth-century novels) with a new acquaintance or a longtime colleague can lead to an exchange of ideas, perspectives, and suggestions—and a promise to continue talking!

In most fields, learning with and from colleagues plays an important role in professional development—too important a role to be left up to chance encounters. Many fields have established structures, tools, and techniques that enable practitioners to interact regularly in ways that promote focused and powerful learning. In the field of education, one such practice that has gained wide popularity over the past 10 years is the use of protocols.

WHAT IS A PROTOCOL?

Protocols are structures that enable educators and, sometimes, others (e.g., parents, invited guests) to look carefully and collaboratively at student and teacher work in order to learn from it. While different protocols vary in significant features, they all do two things: (1) provide a structure for conversation—a series of steps that a group follows in a fixed order, and (2) specify the roles different people in the group will play (typically, a facilitator, a presenter, and participants). Protocols do these things in order to promote a conversation among colleagues that enables them to learn about aspects of teaching and learning. The structure of protocols is intended to encourage conversations, normally carried out within 40 minutes to a little over an hour, that are productive, inclusive, positive, and safe.

Protocols can be deceptively simple. On the surface, it would seem that a group need only walk through the steps of a protocol to have a satisfying conversation. The reality is more complex. Protocols, after all, are designed to help configure—not script—an experience through which individuals and the group as a whole can learn. Experienced teachers know that even with a carefully detailed lesson plan in hand, teaching is not simply about moving through the specified activities one by one. Rather, they use the plan as a guide, while taking into account and responding to the questions, concerns, and responses of the students in the class. The protocol, like the teacher's lesson plan, functions as a guide or an outline. Like any tool, to be useful, it needs to be wielded with skill and good judgment. A facilitator's job, like a teacher's, is not only to know the steps of the protocol, but also to apply the skills and judgment needed to use the protocol effectively to support the group's learning. An experienced facilitator recognizes that the outcomes of such learning experiences are never entirely predictable.

In this chapter, we explore the nature of protocols, the purposes they serve, and the delicate balances they establish in collegial conversation. We are not at this point discussing how to facilitate a protocol. (Chapters 3, 4, and 8 focus more specifically on the responsibilities, skills, and challenges of facilitating a conversation using a protocol.) Rather, we want to suggest productive ways of thinking about protocols. In particular, we consider the following issues:

- The *purposes* of a protocol.
- The *anatomy* of a protocol: the features of a protocol that enable it to accomplish a particular purpose.
- The *spirit* of a protocol: the creative tensions within a group's conversation that protocols help to balance.
- The *authority* of a protocol: the ways in which protocols support facilitators in guiding the conversation.

Two caveats: Throughout this chapter as well as the rest of the book, we use the term "protocol" in two different ways. The first refers to the formal definition of the term: the set of steps that prescribe how a group will interact (e.g., "There are many types of protocols"). The second is a more informal use of the word that designates a particular conversation structured by a protocol ("Last week, in Jim's protocol, we talked about . . .").

Second, while we talk about protocols throughout the book as a key resource for facilitating conversations about students' and teachers' work, this book is not about protocols *per se*. For more detailed treatments of specific protocols, including close descriptions of groups using protocols, see Allen, 1998; Blythe, Allen, & Powell, 1999; Evidence Project Staff, 2001; and McDonald et al., 2003.

THE PURPOSES OF A PROTOCOL

The word *protocol* has different meanings depending on the professional context in which it is used. In education circles, the word has evolved over time to signal a particular kind of group interaction: A protocol-guided conversation aims at enabling educators and interested others to learn more deeply about teaching and learning. Here, and throughout this book, we are speaking of protocols used to promote among colleagues both exploration of important areas of teaching and learning as well as sustained collaborative inquiry into particular questions about teaching and learning. (Chapter 2 details some key differences between protocols and other kinds of professional development.)

Within this broader purpose, different protocols can be used to achieve more specific purposes. The purposes of most protocols in current popular use can be arrayed along a continuum (see Figure 1.1 on page 13) that runs from "question raising/problem finding" to "question answering/problem solving." The Collaborative Assessment Conference protocol (see Figure 1.2 on pages 14–15), for example, would reside at the left side of the purpose continuum as a "question raising/problem finding" protocol. The Tuning Protocol (see Figure 1.3 on pages 16–17), as a structure designed to provide responses to a teacher's specific questions, exemplifies the opposite end of the continuum. The Consultancy (see Figure 1.4 on pages 18–19) blends these two purposes. (All these protocols are discussed in more detail later in this chapter.)

THE ANATOMY OF A PROTOCOL

In large part, the design of the protocol determines whether it will lead the group to finding and exploring open-ended questions or to solving specific problems. Just as the architectural design of a building or the interior design of a room creates certain kinds of possibilities for the inhabitants of that space, so the design of a protocol allows groups to interact in certain ways and to achieve certain ends. In particular, three features of a protocol determine its capacity to promote problem finding, problem solving, or some mix of the two:

- *The role of context.* "Context" here refers to the background information about the work being presented (descriptions of the assignment, the classroom, the students, and so on). In some protocols, the presenting teacher provides a detailed context at the beginning of the conversation. In other protocols, no context is provided until after the participants have discussed the work. In still others, the presenting teacher provides a modest amount of context initially, with more details following in the course of the conversation.
- *The roles of observation, interpretation, and/or evaluation.* Some protocols invite participants to evaluate what they are examining: to point out the strengths and weaknesses of the student work, the clarity of the assignments, and so on. Other protocols never give participants the opportunity to evaluate. Instead, specific steps in these protocols ask participants to describe what they see without resorting to judgments or statements of personal taste. A few protocols ask participants to do both (although usually at different times). And some protocols invite "interpretation" or "speculation"—opportunities to hypothesize about what the student work might signify, for example, about what the student does or does not understand, is trying to achieve or express, or is most interested in.
- *The role of a focusing question.* In some protocols, the presenting teacher is invited to name a specific question that she would like the participants to focus on in their conversation

about the work being examined or her support of the student work and learning. In other protocols, no focusing question, or only a very general one, is invited.

These features are represented on the other three continua in Figure 1.1. As the alignment of the Purposes continuum and the three "Features" continua indicates, protocols with characteristics closer to the left side of the "Features" continua are more likely to help a group explore an aspect of teaching and learning, find and develop questions, and/or identify a problem. Protocols that have features closer to the right side of the continua are typically better suited to helping groups answer questions, solve problems, and focus on specific concerns (such as how to refine a scoring rubric or how well an assignment aligns with the intended learning goals).

Figure 1.1. Purposes and Features of Protocols

Purposes of Protocols

Question Finding	Problem Solving

Features of Protocols

No context provided initially	Some context provided initially	Detailed context provided initially

Observation	Interpretation	Evaluation

No focusing question/issue established	A general focusing question/issue established	A specific focusing question/issue established

Sample Protocols

To illustrate how features influence purpose, we provide brief overviews of several different protocols below. It might be helpful to browse through the protocols themselves (in Figures 1.2–1.4) before reading through the descriptions. As you read about the differences in protocols described in this chapter, you may want to look at protocols not included in this book, including Descriptive Review processes, the ATLAS Protocol, and the Issaquah Coaching Protocol. (For further detail about these protocols, see Allen, 1998; Blythe et al., 1999; Himley & Carini, 2000; McDonald et al., 2003.)

The Collaborative Assessment Conference: A Left-Side Protocol

The Collaborative Assessment Conference (Figure 1.2) typically focuses on an individual piece of student work—one the presenter is genuinely wondering about—in order to promote understanding about that student as a learner and creator within a specific discipline or domain and to spark thinking about teaching and learning issues that

Figure 1.2. The Collaborative Assessment Conference

The Collaborative Assessment Conference
Developed by Steve Seidel and Colleagues at Harvard Project Zero, 1988

Purpose: To give teachers the opportunity to hone their ability to look closely at, articulate questions about, and interpret students' work; to explore the strengths, interests, and needs of a particular student and how an understanding of the individual student can inform next steps in and out of the classroom.

Time: Variable, since steps are not timed. Facilitator uses her judgment in moving the group from one step to the next. The typical protocol usually takes 45–90 minutes.

1. Getting started
   - The group chooses a facilitator who will make sure the group stays focused on the particular issue addressed in each step.
   - The presenting teacher puts the selected work in a place where everyone can see it or provides copies for the other participants. S/he says nothing about the work, the context in which it was created, or the student until Step 5.
   - The participants observe or read the work in silence, perhaps making brief notes about aspects of it that they particularly notice.

2. Describing the work
    - The facilitator asks the group, "What do you see?"
    - Group members provide answers without making judgments about the quality of the work or their personal preferences.
    - If a judgment emerges, the facilitator asks for the evidence on which the judgment is based.

3. Asking questions about the work
    - The facilitator asks the group, "What questions does this work raise for you?"
    - Group members state any questions about the work, the student, the assignment, the circumstances in which the work was carried out, and so on.
    - The presenting teacher may choose to make notes about these questions, but s/he does not respond to them now—nor is s/he obligated to respond to them in Step 5 during the time when s/he speaks.

4. Speculating about what the student is working on
    - The facilitator asks the group, "What do you think the student is working on?"
    - Participants, based on their reading or observation of the work, make suggestions about the problems or issues that the student might have been focused on in carrying out the assignment.

5. Hearing from the presenting teacher
    - The facilitator invites the presenting teacher to speak.
    - The presenting teacher provides his/her perspective on the student's work, describing what s/he sees in it, responding (if s/he chooses) to one or more of the questions raised, and adding any other information that s/he feels is important to share with the group.
    - The presenting teacher also comments on anything surprising or unexpected that s/he heard during the describing, questioning, and speculating phases.

6. Discussing implications for teaching and learning
    - The facilitator invites everyone (the participants and the presenting teacher) to share any thoughts they have about their own teaching, students' learning, or ways to support this particular student in future instruction.

7. Reflecting on the Collaborative Assessment Conference
    - Everyone reflects on the experiences of or reactions to the conference as a whole or to particular parts of it.

8. Thanks to the presenting teacher!

Note: See Chapter 7, Figure 7.1, for more about facilitating the Collaborative Assessment Conference.

apply to other students, classrooms, and disciplines as well. In this protocol, no context is provided initially for the student work being examined by the group. Instead, the presenting teacher provides some of this context at a later point in the protocol. In early steps of the protocol, the group is invited to make observations and interpretations; however, evaluations or judgments are never solicited. Neither the presenting teacher nor the group articulates a focusing question or issue. As a result, the Collaborative Assessment Conference affords groups the opportunity to offer fresh perspectives, raise questions, and explore aspects of teaching and learning generated by the particular student work being examined, without being guided by anyone's "framing" of the work.

The Tuning Protocol: A Right-Side Protocol

The Tuning Protocol (Figure 1.3) typically provides a way for teachers to look closely at their own work in order to "fine-tune" or improve an assignment in light of the student work that has resulted from it. The Tuning Protocol, in contrast to the Collaborative Assessment

Figure 1.3. The Tuning Protocol

The Tuning Protocol
Developed by Joseph McDonald, revised by David Allen
Coalition of Essential Schools, 1991

Purpose: To enable teachers to receive feedback on and fine-tune their assignments, exhibitions, assessment tools, projects, and so on.

Time: Approximately 55–80 minutes

1. Introduction (5 minutes)
   - Facilitator briefly introduces protocol goals, guidelines, and schedule.
   - Participants briefly introduce themselves (if necessary).

2. Presentation (10–15 minutes)
   - The presenter has an opportunity to share the context for the student work, which might include information about the students and/or class, the assignment or prompt, learning goals (or standards) addressed, and evaluation methods used (rubric, scoring criteria, and so on).
   - Presenting teacher frames a focusing question for feedback; facilitator may post focusing question for group to see.
   - Participants are silent; no questions are asked at this time.

3. Clarifying questions (5 minutes)
   - Participants ask "clarifying" questions in order to get information that may have been omitted in the presentation, and that they feel would help them to understand the context for the student work. Clarifying questions are matters of "fact," easily answered by the presenter in a few words.
   - The facilitator should be sure to limit the questions to those that are "clarifying," judging which questions more properly belong in the warm/cool feedback step.

4. Examination of student work samples (10–15 minutes)
   - Participants look closely at the work, keeping the presenter's focusing question in mind, perhaps taking notes for the warm and cool feedback step.
   - Presenter is silent; participants do this work silently or talk quietly with a neighbor.

5. Pause to reflect on warm and cool feedback (2–3 minutes)
   - Participants take a few minutes to reflect individually on what they would like to contribute to the feedback session.
   - Presenter is silent.

6. Warm and cool feedback (10–15 minutes)
   - Participants share feedback with one another while the presenter listens. The feedback typically begins with a few minutes of warm feedback, moves on to a few minutes of cool feedback, and then a mix of the two.
   - *Warm feedback* points to strengths—for example, comments about how the work presented seems to meet the desired goals. *Cool feedback* identifies possible "disconnects," or gaps, between the work and the teacher's goals for it; cool feedback often is phrased as a question.
   - The facilitator may need to remind participants of the presenter's focusing question.
   - Presenter is silent; s/he may choose to take notes.

7. Reflection (5–10 minutes)
   - Presenter addresses those comments/questions s/he chooses to. The purpose is not to defend the student work or his/her own work, but instead to reflect aloud on those ideas or questions that seemed particularly compelling or intriguing.
   - Facilitator may intervene to help focus, clarify, and so on.
   - Participants listen silently.

8. Debrief (5–10 minutes)
   - Facilitator leads discussion focused on the process, rather than content, of the discussion—i.e., how the protocol supported a learning conversation.
   - Everyone participates.

Note: See Chapter 7, Figure 7.1, for more about facilitating the Tuning Protocol.

Conference, bears the features of the right side of the continua: The protocol opens with the presenting teacher providing a fairly detailed description of the context in which the student work was generated as well as, perhaps, some information about the students who created the work. In addition, the teacher usually provides a "focusing question" (see Chapter 5) to which she would like the group to attend. Evaluation, in the form of "warm" and "cool" feedback, is explicitly requested of group members. The Tuning Protocol, then, provides groups with the opportunity to focus on specific issues articulated by the presenting teacher and to offer feedback in response to the questions she has framed.

The Consultancy: Somewhere in the Middle

The Consultancy (Figure 1.4) was developed initially as part of the Coalition of Essential Schools' Re:Learning Program and was adapted and further developed by Gene Thompson-Grove and colleagues at the National School Reform Faculty. It offers educators the opportunity to share a dilemma with colleagues in order to explore other perspectives and ways of thinking about that dilemma. This protocol includes a mix of right-side and left-side features. At the beginning of the protocol, the presenting teacher describes her dilemma, normally including a focusing question. She then responds to the group's clarifying questions

Figure 1.4. The Consultancy

The Consultancy
Originally developed as part of the Coalition of Essential Schools'
National Re:Learning Faculty Program; further adapted
and revised by Gene Thompson-Grove and colleagues in the
National School Reform Faculty

Purpose: A Consultancy is a structured process for helping an individual or a team think more expansively about a particular, concrete dilemma from his/her classroom/professional life.

Time: Approximately 50 minutes

1. Presentation of the dilemma (5–10 minutes)
   - The presenter gives an overview of the dilemma with which s/he is struggling and frames a question for the Consultancy group to consider. The framing of

this question, as well as the quality of the presenter's reflection on the dilemma being discussed, are key features of this protocol. If the presenter has brought student work, educator work, or other "artifacts," there is a pause here to silently examine the work/documents. The focus of the group's conversation is on the dilemma.

2. Clarifying questions (5 minutes)
   - The Consultancy group asks clarifying questions of the presenter—that is, questions that have brief, factual answers.

3. Probing questions (10 minutes)
   - The group asks probing questions of the presenter. These questions should be worded so that they help the presenter clarify and expand his/her thinking about the dilemma presented to the Consultancy group. The goal here is for the presenter to learn more about the question s/he framed or to do some analysis of the dilemma presented. The presenter may respond to the group's questions, but there is no discussion by the Consultancy group of the presenter's responses. At the end of the 10 minutes, the facilitator asks the presenter to restate his/her question for the group.

4. Discussion of the dilemma (15 minutes)
   - The group members talk with one another about the dilemma presented. Possible questions to frame the discussion:
     What did we hear?
     What didn't we hear that we think might be relevant?
     What assumptions seem to be operating?
     What questions does the dilemma raise for us?
     What do we think about the dilemma?
     What might we do or try if faced with a similar dilemma?
     What have we done in similar situations?
   - Members of the group sometimes suggest solutions to the dilemma. Most often, however, they work to define the issues more thoroughly and objectively. The presenter doesn't speak during this discussion, but listens and takes notes.

5. Presenter reflection (5 minutes)
   - The presenter reflects on what s/he heard and on what s/he is now thinking, sharing with the group anything that particularly resonated for him/her during any part of the Consultancy.

6. Debrief (5 minutes)
   - The facilitator leads a brief conversation about the group's observation of the Consultancy process.

Note: See Chapter 7, Figure 7.1, for more about facilitating the Consultancy.

about the dilemma or focusing question. The two steps together provide the group with a fairly detailed context as well as a specific focus for the conversation—both right-side features. In the ensuing conversation, participants are invited to think specifically about the presenter's dilemma and focusing question, and also to offer their own perspectives on and ideas about the problem. While no evaluation is expressly invited, neither is it prohibited, and the resulting conversation usually provides a mix of problem finding and problem solving. The Consultancy, then, tends to yield a blend of possible solutions to current dilemmas as well as some new questions to puzzle about.

Given these key differences in purpose and structure among various protocols, the facilitator must help the group and the presenting teacher choose the protocol that will be most productive. In Chapter 8, we provide a more thorough discussion of this process.

THE SPIRIT OF A PROTOCOL

A well-designed protocol is more than the sum of its steps. Protocols not only have specific and identifiable features and goals, but they also have a certain "feel" or create a certain atmosphere in which a group works together. Often, the spirit of a protocol is generated by the ways in which the various steps work together to maintain a creative tension among several important qualities. These tensions are briefly described below.

Talking and Listening

Protocols designate times for talking and listening. For example, the group speaks while the presenting teacher listens; later, the presenting teacher talks while the group listens without interrupting. Some protocols also provide times when everyone talks (and, one hopes, listens!) together.

Discipline and Play

Different protocols offer different degrees of balance between requiring a specific kind of response from group members and allowing for more open conversation. For example, participants might be asked to limit themselves in one step to making only purely descriptive comments about the work, or to concentrate on naming particular strengths in the work. A different step might invite open, free-flowing responses that allow for more play, in both senses of the word: more elbow room for introducing varied types of questions and comments, as well as more playfulness in speculation or wondering out loud about the work. This is one of the fulcrum points for which "balance" suggests a directly proportional relationship, rather than an inverse one: The more discipline a protocol requires, the more play it can support as well (although at different times during the protocol, of course).

Safety and Risk

As in any learning situation, too much safety is lulling, perhaps even boring; too much risk is threatening. Different protocols offer various mixes of safety for the group and the presenting teacher (in the form of predictability, for example, or by requiring the group to withhold judgment of the presenting teacher's work) and risk (in the form of opportunities to open up central, sometimes controversial or sensitive issues of teaching and learning or opportunities to have one's assumptions challenged by the differing perspectives of others).

Individual Learning and Group Learning

Protocols afford opportunities for both individual and group learning, although often one or the other is emphasized. For example, in some protocols, the presenting teacher decides the focus of the conversation, and most of the group energy is spent supporting her in learning about the issue or the question that she has named. Of course, other participants in the group also will benefit in some way from this discussion, often making powerful connections with their own teaching and students' learning. In other protocols, particularly ones in which the presenting teacher does not get to name the focusing question, the focus of the conversation emerges from and is explored by the group (although, of course, the presenting teacher also learns important things in the course of such discussions).

*   *   *

By "balance," we do not mean the static, steady state of a set of scales weighted equally. Think instead of a dynamic fluctuation, perhaps the way a pendulum maintains a kind of balance by swinging back and forth over a single midpoint. The balances described here shift throughout a protocol. Different protocols provide for different balances. For example, one protocol may encourage more listening on the part of the presenting teacher; another may hold the group in the listening role for longer or at different points. The facilitator plays a critical role in finding and maintaining the right balance, although, as we discuss in the next section, the protocol itself can serve as a partner in this work. The group also shares the responsibility for getting the balance right. Its ability to do so, of course, hinges on the participants' understanding of the protocol—understanding that comes through both experience and the facilitator's work with the group.

THE AUTHORITY OF A PROTOCOL

On the surface, a protocol is a useful tool for setting out the steps for a group's conversation. In a subtler way, protocols are more than mere tools. The protocols themselves carry a certain amount of authority in a group. Many facilitators, especially relatively new ones, describe relying on the presence of the protocol when they face particular challenges—for example, in needing to interrupt an exchange in order to move their colleagues from one step to the next. ("Lots of ideas have come up in the last few minutes—I wish we could keep talking, but according to the protocol, at this point we need to move on to the next step.")

In this way, the protocol functions as a kind of co-facilitator—another guide for the process. Protocols (like facilitators) all come with a certain amount of experience, from the relatively inexperienced, newly devised protocol to the very experienced stalwarts such as the Tuning Protocol or the Collaborative Assessment Conference. Furthermore, in using a protocol over time, group members begin to develop trust in it: Even when participants can't be sure where a conversation is headed or how to tackle a particularly challenging piece of student work, they can respond willingly to the invitation extended by the protocol to engage with the work and one another with confidence that following the protocol will result in a productive conversation.

For participants in groups using protocols, the use of protocols is a discipline akin to meditation or physical exercise. Regular practice is important. The use of protocols is never mastered overnight. It takes time for both facilitators and group members to develop familiarity and comfort with the skills and habits a protocol requires. Progress emerges over time rather than within a session or two. Both facilitator and participants need to understand that using a protocol is not a simple solution, but rather a practice that, over time, harnesses the power of collaboration to support the learning of groups as well as individuals.

BEYOND THE PROTOCOL

We've begun our discussion in this book by focusing on protocols. In subsequent chapters (as the book title promises), we will move to an emphasis on facilitation. However, neither a good protocol nor skilled facilitation can guarantee a productive discussion. Protocol-guided conversations are more complex than that. In addition to the protocol and the facilitation, at least four other points of influence determine the effectiveness of a conversation:

- *The group participants*: their level of experience with protocols in general or with the particular protocol being used; their comfort with one another; their willingness to take risks; their level of commitment to their own and the group's learning; and so on.
- *The presenter*: her level of experience with the particular protocol being used or with protocols in general; the degree to which she is able to identify and willing to share a question or issue that concerns her about her own teaching or students' learning; the degree to which she is able to listen to the group and respond without defensiveness to their observations and critique.
- *The work*: the degree to which samples of student and/or teacher work make visible the teacher's and/or students' thinking and learning; the degree to which the work has been selected to "show off" or to represent or illustrate a real question,

issue, or dilemma; the amount, format, and range of work samples; and so on.
- *The question or issue framed by the presenter and/or the group*:
  the degree to which the question or issue feels important or
  urgent to the presenter and/or group members; the opportunities the question and/or issue opens up for group members
  to make connections to and among their own experiences.

All this complexity can, in some ways, be reassuring: No one person
or element holds sole responsibility for the success of a protocol-guided conversation. A powerful and compelling question can compensate
for a reticent presenter or work that doesn't seem to reveal much about
the students who carried it out. A committed and enthusiastic group
can support an inexperienced or hesitant facilitator. Both protocol-
guided conversations that go well and those that seem less satisfying
need to be considered in light of all of these factors. (Chapter 8 explores
in more depth the challenges related to these factors.)

Chapter 2

How Are Protocols Different from Other Kinds of Professional Development?

In Chapter 1, we presented a way of distinguishing protocols from one another. Facilitators also need to consider how protocol-guided conversation (whatever the actual protocol used) differs from other forms of professional development, particularly those forms with which group members are likely to be more familiar. With an understanding of the ways in which using protocols is both similar to and different from other kinds of professional learning experiences, facilitators can help participants appreciate the unique features of protocols and how to most profitably take part in them.

Most professional development for teachers falls into one of three categories: (1) direct instruction, (2) mentoring/coaching, and (3) collegial conversation and reflection (Bray et al., 2000; Killion & Simmons, 1992).

- *Direct instruction*: Workshops, university courses, training sessions for particular types of curriculum, instructional strategies, and technology use exemplify this kind of professional development.
- *Mentoring/coaching*: In this kind of professional development, a teacher typically works one-on-one with a more experienced educator. The mentor provides direct, individual feedback to the teacher about ways in which she might improve her practice.
- *Collegial conversation and reflection*: Critical friends groups, teacher inquiry groups, and groups that use protocols to look at student and teacher work are examples of this kind of professional development.

No one of these approaches is superior to any other: Adults, just as students, require different kinds of learning opportunities to improve their skills and understanding. Each of these three types of professional development has the potential to contribute something valuable to teacher growth and development.

In most school districts, direct instruction is the predominant mode of professional development. Some school districts develop individual coaching and mentoring systems. The number of school districts that support collegial conversation as a form of professional development has grown steadily over the past 10 years; yet it still remains the least familiar and least supported of the three modes of professional development.

WHAT'S SO SPECIAL ABOUT PROTOCOLS?

Why should this imbalance in professional development experiences be a problem? We argue in this chapter that collegial conversation, particularly when guided by protocols, offers a learning environment with unique features, and therefore unique opportunities for the growth of understanding and professional skill and judgment. In particular, we consider how protocols differ from more prevalent forms of professional development in terms of how expertise and control are situated, and, ultimately, how they differ in their underlying "theory of change." These variations are summarized in Figure 2.1.

Locus of Control

One key difference among forms of professional development, whether a protocol, workshop, or coaching session, is in who decides the focus and content of the meeting.

Even when a school or district requests a particular kind of workshop (e.g., a workshop on assessment or learning styles), typically it is the workshop leader who determines the particular learning goals that are reasonable to achieve, as well as the kinds of activities that will best help participants attain those goals.

Mentoring or coaching relationships involve a bit more negotiation. The mentor or coach might have certain ideas, based on her observa-

Figure 2.1. Approaches to Professional Development

Workshop/ Training	Coaching/ Mentoring	Collegial Conversation/ Inquiry Groups

Locus of Control

Workshop Leader/ Expert	Coach and Coached	Participants

Locus of Expertise

Workshop Leader/ Expert	Coach and Coached	Participants

**Theory of Change:
How does each approach aim to improve student learning**

Learn techniques/strategies, then use them in the classroom	Practice a strategy/technique with ongoing feedback	Develop a deeper understanding of student learning in order to develop/ decide on new strategies and techniques for the classroom

tions of the teacher being coached, about the issues the coached teacher most needs to focus on. Just as often, however, the teacher being coached is likely to say, "What I need right now is help with . . . ." In collegial conversations, especially protocols, the group itself usually determines the goals for the conversation and how the members will pursue those goals. The goals may reflect school-wide focus areas; however, such focus areas typically are interpreted, or "customized," by the group. While an experienced outside facilitator might provide ideas or advice, the participants themselves ultimately must take responsibility for setting and achieving the goals that are most important to them.

Locus of Expertise

Another important way in which the three forms of professional development differ is in where the expertise is seen to reside. In the case of a workshop or graduate course, the workshop leader or course instructor typically is viewed as the "expert" who, by virtue of her greater skill and experience in a particular area, can enable participants to develop their own expertise or skills in that area. Similarly, in coaching, educators with more expertise typically serve as mentors for less experienced teachers. However, the mentored person is assumed to have some developing expertise about her own situation and her own professional needs.

The special province of protocols is in creating a space in which all participants, by virtue of their experience—no matter what that experience is—can make important contributions to the conversation and, consequently, to the group's learning. To borrow a "norm" adopted by some groups, there is "no monopoly on expertise." In the collaborative deliberation of the group, moments of insight, powerful questions, and intriguing suggestions are as likely to emerge from the reflections of a student teacher as from a 20-year veteran. They are as likely to come from colleagues who teach different grade levels or subject matters as from those working in the same discipline or grade level. Using protocols as an approach to professional development honors the wealth of expertise that already exists within a school or group of educators. It gives educators a collegial context in which to share and further develop their own expertise while supporting the growth of others.

One might argue that the same could be said of a well-run workshop: A good workshop leader would value all participants' comments equally and would take seriously their experiences and validate those experiences. The leader might even turn to the group at points throughout the workshop to invite them to make decisions about which topics to cover next, whether to spend more time on a particular issue, and so on. However, in such a setting, inevitably the leader still holds the position of expert with respect to the topic being discussed. In fact, usually a workshop leader has been asked to lead the workshop precisely because the group expects that she has more expertise in a particular area than anyone else in the room.

Similarly, teachers usually sign up to take a course with a particular instructor because they feel they can learn something that they otherwise would not be able to master on their own. Furthermore, while course instructors or workshop leaders might well ask participants what they would like to learn, most typically the instructors or leaders use this information to modify the goals they have already identified, not to replace them.

The learning that happens in a protocol comes as a result of the group's collaborative work within a certain structure, not because the facilitator is an expert who can instruct the group on a given topic. If the facilitator intends a protocol to lead the group to "discover" what she already knows or, for that matter, what the presenter or anyone else in the group already knows, the possibility for genuine group learning is negated from the start. Imagine a facilitator who proposes to her group a series of Tuning Protocols in order to consider how a particular content or performance standard could be addressed in teachers' curricula and instruction. If the facilitator's proposal is driven by the belief that, through the protocol, she can teach participants how to apply the standards, we would argue that the "protocol" is then a workshop disguised as a protocol. If, on the other hand, the purpose of the protocol is for participants to come together as peers, each with experience, perspectives, and questions to share, in order to learn how to enact the standards more effectively—and if the facilitator is there to support that conversation without presuming special expertise on the topic—then a true protocol—that is, a true collaborative learning experience—can unfold.

None of this is to deny the importance of workshops or classes for helping teachers to learn certain kinds of skills and content: how to plan a lesson, how to use new technology in the school, how to set up a specific disciplinary routine, and so on. If the goal is to learn CPR, for example, a Collaborative Assessment Conference would be a poor substitute for a training conducted by a skilled medical practitioner.

However, teachers (like all professionals) also need opportunities to reflect on their lived experience, to check their perceptions and assumptions against those of other professionals, and to identify the needs and goals for their own learning. They need opportunities for what Clark (2001) calls "authentic conversations" in which colleagues learn from one another through making their implicit theories and beliefs explicit, affirming ideals and commitments, taking on new perspectives, and developing a sense of personal and professional authority. Protocols offer teachers opportunities for these essential learning experiences.

Theory of Change

Different theories of change underlie each approach. The theory that drives the workshop/course model might be: Learning a new strategy or technique leads to changes in teaching practice, which lead to improved student learning. For the coaching model the theory might be: Practicing a strategy or technique with ongoing feedback leads to changes in practice, which lead to improved student learning. The theory for protocols might be: Looking collaboratively and carefully at the work happening in their own classrooms leads teachers to deepen their understanding of that work through hearing others' perspectives and questions about it, which leads to the teachers developing new teaching approaches based on that understanding, which leads to changes in their classroom practice, which leads to improved student learning.

All of these theories have contexts in which they seem to work well. Nevertheless, it is worth noting that the "chain" stretching from the structured professional development experience to improved practice and improved student learning is longest in the case of protocols. For this reason, the time that this kind of professional development takes to yield improved student learning may be longer as well. However, teachers who have used protocols over time report significant changes in practice, and preliminary findings of research that follows such work over a period of a year or more are similarly encouraging (Little, Gearhart, Curry, & Kafka, 2003; Weinbaum et al., 2004).

WHAT DOES THIS MEAN FOR
THE FACILITATOR'S ROLE IN A PROTOCOL?

These differences have significant implications for the facilitator's role. In collegial conversations, the facilitator does not provide special expertise about the content of the conversation. Her role is to guide the process and to help people use the protocol well—not to help the group come to the "right" or "best" (in the facilitator's opinion) understanding of the topic or issue being discussed. The facilitator's main commitment is to the process and the group's learning. She may well intervene in a protocol, but that intervention needs to be in the service of encouraging other perspectives as the protocol invites them—not of asserting her own perspective as the correct one.

This is not to suggest that a facilitator does not have powerful beliefs about what constitutes good student work or good teaching practice. However, the beliefs that most influence her work as a facilitator have to do with what makes for good collegial conversation (e.g., a belief that student work is a powerful source of evidence of the teaching and learning in a classroom; or a belief that collegial dialogue about specific problems and pieces of work is the best way for professionals to identify their own assumptions and potential misconceptions; and so on). Facilitators need to reflect on their beliefs about protocols and articulate them for the group. At the same time, we believe that a facilitator must take care not to interject into the conversation her beliefs about what constitutes good teaching and learning unless she can be reasonably certain the group will not give her contributions special weight because of her role as the facilitator.

Because many educators are most familiar with other models of professional development (workshops, coaching) in which a leader *does* bring and share special content expertise, the idea of the facilitator as a moderator of the process rather than the content may be difficult initially for some to grasp. Participants may believe that the facilitator does in fact have—or should have—the answers to questions that emerge. They may even be disappointed to realize that the facilitator does not have such answers. As a result, some may question the value of the conversation. Facilitators need to resist consistently this subtle pressure to "be the expert" if the protocol is to provide real opportunities for group learning. See Chapter 8 for some ways a facilitator might respond when participants turn to her (or another participant) as an expert on the content, rather than the process.

But what if the protocol-guided conversations of a group seem never to address issues that the facilitator herself feels are essential to good teaching and learning? What if the facilitator feels that the conversations are not substantive or deep enough? David Green, an expert on school quality review visits, warns reviewers to be open to "the infuriating success of the 'wrong' methods." We would say the same of protocol facilitators: It may well be that the group is not progressing, that the conversations are not yielding useful learning for the group members. But before a facilitator can make such a determination, she must consider well and carefully the degree to which she truly understands the kind of learning that is developing for a group in its current conversations.

Clues about the kinds of learning actually taking place are not always obvious in the conversation. And learning in the more open-ended conversations of a protocol (as opposed to a workshop setting with its more narrowly defined learning goals) can take a huge and complex variety of forms—rarely just those that the facilitator, or anyone else, would have predicted: Combing the beach exclusively to find the rare bits of blue sea glass, one could well miss the hundreds of other beautiful shells and rocks the waves have washed up. In Chapters 3 and 4, we consider how, through "debriefing" and reflecting, facilitators and the groups they work with assess progress without giving up on process.

A facilitator needs to maintain a commitment to a protocol and a belief in that protocol's capacity to create a space where the group members can learn together in ways that no one of them could learn individually. To the degree that the facilitator participates in the substance of the protocol at all, it must be with a voice and a set of experiences that are no more "privileged" than any other voice in the conversation. Otherwise, she undermines the possibility that the group may generate some question or learning or understanding that is truly the group's (not the facilitator's, bestowed upon the group) and uniquely relevant to the group members, their context, and their set of concerns. That possibility is, we believe, the true contribution of protocols to the professional development of educators.

Chapter 3

What Do Facilitators Do?
The Big Picture

Effective protocols are not simply a matter of what happens from the time the protocol starts until it ends. For protocols to be effective learning tools, facilitators need to attend to at least three broad areas of concern. In this chapter, we will introduce those major areas of responsibilities. We will also discuss the key "thinking dispositions" that facilitators need to cultivate in order to carry out their roles effectively.

FACILITATING LEARNING, LOGISTICS, AND LONGEVITY

To make protocols powerful learning opportunities, facilitators need to attend (or see that someone else attends) to three areas of responsibility:

- The learning of the group
- The logistics of meetings
- The longevity of the work within the school or district

These areas are represented in the circles of Figure 3.1 and are discussed in more detail below. As the arrangement of the circles demonstrates, these are overlapping spheres, and some responsibilities are found in more than one.

Facilitating Learning

Fundamentally, protocols are about providing all participants with the opportunity to learn both as individuals and as a group. Facilitators

Figure 3.1. Facilitating Learning, Logistics, and Longevity

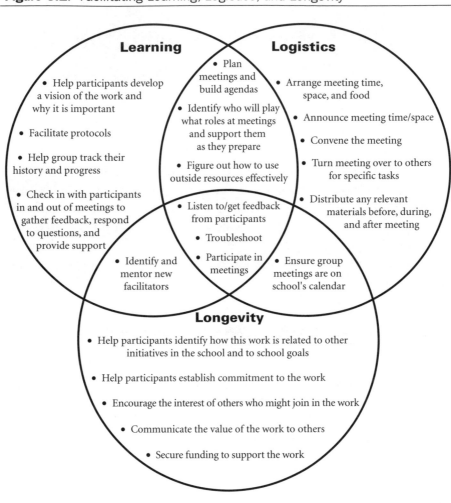

Note: Adapted from *The Evidence Process: A Collaborative Approach to Understanding and Improving Teaching and Learning* by the Evidence Project Staff (Cambridge, MA: Harvard Project Zero, 2001).

concentrate before, during, and after meetings on shaping the process to enhance this. In this role, facilitators address key responsibilities such as

- helping participants in the group develop their understanding of the purpose for their collaborative work

- helping the group understand how its process, including the use of protocols, helps achieve its purpose(s)
- facilitating protocols that give participants the chance to learn together
- helping the group track its evolving learning by documenting its work and helping the group reflect on that work from time to time
- checking in with participants in and out of meetings to gather feedback, respond to questions, and provide support

Facilitating Logistics

As with any group meeting, logistical details in those meetings that include protocols require attention. Simply put, someone has to handle the nuts and bolts of the work: Where will the group meet? Who will make sure the materials are there (the student work photocopied, the chart paper in place, and so on)? Who will make sure everyone knows where to go and what time to be there? Who will arrange for the refreshments? A big part of facilitating logistics is communicating before and after meetings with participants in the group (and others playing supporting roles in and out of the school).

Facilitating Longevity

Learning, whether it happens individually or with a group, takes time. And using protocols as a tool for learning takes practice in order for groups to engage in them effectively. If a group is to reap the full benefit of protocol-guided conversation, then it needs to meet and use protocols on a regular basis. This can't happen without specific attention being given to issues such as

- helping participants identify how this work is related to other initiatives in the school and to school goals
- helping participants establish commitment to the work
- encouraging the interest of others who might join in the work
- communicating the value of this work to others in the school and outside of the school
- securing funding to support the work

Usually, an administrator will play a key role in facilitating longevity. This role will be best served if she is familiar with all aspects of the group's learning and logistics, and is in close communication with the facilitator(s).

Overlapping Responsibilities

In practice, these roles overlap. For example, in talking with the presenting teacher before a meeting, the facilitator usually helps the presenter frame a problem or question to focus the group's discussion— an important step in facilitating learning (see Chapter 7). However, she also may go over more logistical details, such as copying materials, how to set up the room, and so on.

Of course, no one person should carry out all these roles alone. Two or three people (from inside the group and/or from a partner organization) can share these roles regularly. Occasionally, others in the group can take on some of these responsibilities as well. Such division of labor can help avoid the all-too-familiar feeling of being overwhelmed and getting "burned out." It also can spread the wealth, in terms of opportunities to learn about facilitation and practicing facilitation skills.

A reality check: At least in getting started, a primary facilitator often takes on the lion's share of facilitating learning and logistics, as well as communicating frequently with school leadership about longevity issues. Over time, the facilitator, school leaders, outside partner(s), and participants in the group should revisit and re-evaluate how these roles can be shared.

FACILITATORS' "THINKING DISPOSITIONS":
READING, RESPONDING, AND REFLECTING

In whichever area of responsibility facilitators work (facilitating learning, logistics, or longevity), they need to cultivate key skills. We call these skills "thinking dispositions," drawing on the work of David Perkins, Shari Tishman, and others at Harvard Project Zero. "Thinking dispositions" embrace more than the actual skills: To have a particular thinking disposition (such as the disposition to examine assumptions), one must have not only the skill to carry out the task, but also the sensitivity to recognize when that skill is useful and the motivation to use it at the appropriate times (Tishman, Perkins, & Jay, 1995). Like all thinking dispositions, the ones we name here can be nurtured and deepened over time through practice and reflection (see Chapter 9).

The three dispositions we discuss in this chapter—reading, responding, and reflecting—are less visible than the specific actions a facilitator might take in a protocol. However, these dispositions play a critical role in the facilitator's ability to organize, select, develop, and employ specific actions in particular situations. (These specific actions, which many facilitators refer to as "moves," are considered in Chapter 4.) While each of these dispositions is useful in each of the three major areas of responsibility, we will concentrate in the remainder of this chapter on the sphere of "facilitating learning." In particular, we will focus on how these dispositions are useful in guiding protocols.

Reading the Group and the Situation: What's Going On?

While facilitators must read materials (the protocol, the student work, and so on), this disposition refers to a more figurative kind of reading. Just as a football team's quarterback or a basketball team's point guard must be able to "read" the field or court, the facilitator must be able to take in and make sense of what is going on within the conversation as it unfolds in order to make decisions about what to do at any given moment (including the decision to do nothing at all) to best support the group's learning. This disposition actually consists of several component dispositions, including listening, observing, and asking for the group's "read" of the situation.

Listening

While most protocols designate specific periods in which either the participants or the presenter listens while others speak, the facilitator must listen actively and intently throughout the entire conversation. But what, precisely, does a facilitator listen for? It begs the question to say "anything and everything," so instead we offer this necessarily incomplete list:

- What may be unclear to the presenter, a participant, or the group (about the protocol, their role, or the content of the conversation)?

- What may be general or abstract (in the focusing question, the presenter's presentation, or a participant's question or feedback)?
- What may be judgmental or evaluative (when evaluation is not called for or intentionally excluded)?
- What may detract from the group's focus (e.g., storytelling or "story-topping," such as, "I know what you mean, I once had a student who . . .")?
- What may be out of place (i.e., would be better offered in a different part of the protocol)?
- What contributions may provide helpful examples to point out to the group (e.g., a "probing question" or descriptive comment)?
- What may indicate an emerging focus of interest for the group (in participants' questions or during the feedback discussion)?

All of these questions begin with the construction, "What may . . . ." This hedging is deliberate. Without knowing the context and variables— the group, its purposes and style of working, the presenter's interests or question, the protocol being used, the specific point in the conversation, and so on—it is impossible to judge whether a comment is too general or abstract (perhaps an abstraction is just what the group needs at that moment to stimulate its thinking), when a story or anecdote is going to advance the conversation or distract from its goal, and so on.

For facilitators, this disposition means more than just listening for unclear, misplaced, or off-topic contributions in order to somehow correct or censor them. (Facilitators are almost always able to encourage participants to rephrase or "redirect" comments; see Chapter 4.) Listening also involves identifying emerging ideas or questions and highlighting them for the group's consideration, as well as identifying particular comments or questions that can help participants appreciate how a specific part of the protocol may be used effectively.

Observing

In reading the group, the facilitator is not, as in football, sizing up a defense to find a little daylight. There is no defense or offense in protocols! However, she is constantly monitoring the group to determine how well the conversation is achieving its broader purpose of being a learning opportunity for all participants, as well as meeting more specific goals the presenter and the group have framed. Just as a facilitator listens for indicators of understanding or confusion in what is said, she also pays close attention to what other kinds of signals can reveal, for example, about a participant's (or the group's) needs, understanding of the process, or comfort level with certain kinds of questions or comments.

Sometimes specific actions or expressions of body language are readily translatable. For example, when participants look up after having examined closely the samples of work, they probably are signaling they've had enough time to look at the work. Other expressions of body language may be more difficult to read. For example, when, after a participant's clarifying question, the presenter turns to the facilitator, lifts an eyebrow and shrugs her shoulders, is she asking whether she should answer, suggesting she doesn't know how to answer, or signaling discomfort with the question itself?

Sometimes a constellation of observable signals can help the facilitator read the mood of the group. For example, if two participants at one end of the table begin a quiet "side conversation," others start to straighten the papers in front of them, and the participant next to the facilitator checks his watch, it's likely the group is restless and ready to move on. However, facilitators should not to be overly influenced by more expressive or dramatic participants' comments or body language. The facilitator might want to pay special attention to participants who may be more difficult to read, present themselves more passively, or may require more time or a second invitation to contribute to the conversation.

Asking for the Group's "Read"

Careful listening and observing allow the facilitator to make informed decisions about what kind of response, if any, is most appropriate. However, the facilitator does not have to rely solely on what she herself hears or observes. She often can ask the group for their perspectives before making a judgment about what steps she should take.

Facilitators sometimes refer to such inquiries as "process questions," and may choose to name them as such for the group: "I'd like to ask a process question at this point." For example, if the facilitator

cannot determine whether a presenter's glance and body language signal discomfort with the question or confusion about the process, she
simply may ask the presenter, "Is that a question you can answer easily in a sentence or two, or should I suggest we take it up later in the
conversation?"

Asking such questions invites the participants and the presenter to
share with the facilitator the responsibility for the conversation. Of
course, facilitators ask many other kinds of questions, as we will see in
considering the other facilitation dispositions below and facilitation
"moves" in Chapter 4.

Responding: What (If Anything) Should I Do?

Reading the group allows the facilitator to pick up on potential
problems and emerging opportunities. Of course, in a protocol, everybody is expected to be responsive (as well as attentive) to the presenter,
one another, and whatever student or teacher work may be presented.
However, only the facilitator is specifically charged with responding in
order to ensure that the process is productive, inclusive, and safe for all
participants. While the participants can pay attention to the individual
trees, the facilitator must attend to the forest as well.

A facilitator's response (or decision not to respond) is a direct
result of her reading of the group. Many facilitators talk about these
responses as "moves." The purposes of these moves are many: to pick
up or slow down the pace of conversation, to help clarify steps of the
protocol or comments that participants have made, to encourage
participants to anchor their comments in the evidence provided by
the work being examined, and so on. Chapter 4 describes some of the
more common moves that facilitators make in responding. At this
point, it is useful to take up a question that is always present in a
facilitator's enactment of her role: When do I step in?

Like classroom teachers, facilitators make decisions nearly every
moment of their group's discussion. Often they make a decision to
intervene—saying or doing something to affect the situation that is
developing. Just as often, they elect not to intervene, judging that it is
better to let the discussion unfold on its own (aware, perhaps, that
intervention may be called for at some point in the near future). This
"negative" response can open up space for reflection, questioning, or

interactions to occur that might have been constrained by an intervention from the facilitator.

In protocols, facilitators recognize that too little response could allow the conversation to become unfocused or allow a potentially detrimental comment to affect the tone of the group; on the other hand, too much—or poorly timed—response brings the risk of disrupting the flow of conversation or putting too much focus on the facilitator, rather than on the presenter and the group.

Facilitators navigate between these two poles in different ways. Simply being aware of them, and the risks of hewing too closely to either, may help a facilitator monitor her own facilitation. In more novice groups, facilitators may find themselves responding or intervening more often, but even the most experienced group benefits from a well-timed question or reminder. Some facilitators find value in the maxim, "She who responds least, responds best"; however, all facilitators must be prepared to intervene, even when it is not always comfortable to do so. Through experience, facilitators find their own most productive ways of responding.

Reflecting: What Went On and What Can Be Learned from It?

So far, the dispositions of facilitation we have discussed have called for a heightened awareness of what is happening within the conversation and within the group, and a readiness to respond *in the moment*. In a sense, "reading" asks the facilitator to pay close attention to the forest, as well as the individual trees; and "responding" requires her to look for alternative paths through the forest.

However, good facilitators also value stepping back from the action and reflecting on a protocol once it is over. The disposition of reflecting, then, asks the facilitator to adopt a bird's-eye perspective that allows her to look out over the forest, trees, and paths, and consider how the group worked its way through the forest together and how decisions made by the facilitator herself at key moments affected their journey, particularly in supporting the participants' opportunities for learning.

In looking back over a learning conversation, the facilitator also is looking forward to the next one, in which she might try something different (e.g., being sure to ask people to point to specific evidence in their feedback) and pay close attention to what happens when she does. She also may commit herself to being more aware of tendencies she has noticed in the group or in herself (e.g., asking, "Am I saying too much in setting up parts of the protocol?") and being prepared to respond to them.

The facilitator's reflection on a learning conversation may begin when she invites the group to "debrief" the conversation they've just had (a typical step at the end of most protocols). Having follow-up conversations with group members outside of the protocol setting also can be extremely valuable in supporting thoughtful reflection, as can talking to other, perhaps more experienced, facilitators about the group's progress.

Documentation of the group's work and learning is another important tool for a facilitator's reflections. Documentation that captures aspects of the conversation (through notes or "minutes," journals, or even occasional audio or video recordings) provides a basis for individual and group reflection. In Chapter 4, we consider some of the strategies facilitators use for documenting conversations and drawing on that documentation. In the final chapter, we take a more sustained look at how facilitators reflect on their own development.

Facilitation Style

Although it is not a disposition, the issue of style bears some mention here. If one watched videos of two facilitators in two separate protocols, one would find them maintaining the same thinking dispositions, perhaps even making nearly identical moves, yet their facilitation might appear to be very different. Some facilitators, for example, are more inclined to be explicit about following a protocol, adhering strictly to its steps and announcing each step as the group moves through it. Others follow the protocol more implicitly, moving from step to step without much overt "cueing" of the group. Some facilitators inject humor to ease transitions, to help the group get comfortable with one another, or to diffuse potentially uncomfortable moments. For others, using humor in this way would feel forced: They find other ways to help groups move through tense situations and to work together productively and positively.

There is no such thing as a "correct" facilitation style. Perhaps the only recommendation we would make here is to encourage facilitators to experiment consciously with different approaches and to be aware of the impact those different approaches seem to have on the group's work. In Chapter 9, we discuss how facilitators learn not only from one another's specific moves, but from one another's styles as well.

Chapter 4

What Do Facilitators Do in a Protocol?

In the previous chapter, we described three roles (facilitating learning, logistics, and longevity) and three thinking dispositions (reading, responding, and reflecting) that are germane to the work of a facilitator. In this chapter, we will focus more specifically on protocols themselves and what a facilitator does while guiding the group through one.

While protocols lay out clear steps for a conversation, facilitators often find themselves intervening in ways that go beyond merely walking a group through the process. They might clarify steps, redirect the conversation when it veers off track, summarize particular parts of the conversation before moving the group on to the next step, and so on. Protocols typically do not contain the script for such actions. Rather, facilitators use their judgment and experience in deciding when to act and what to say. Facilitators often refer to these unscripted actions as "moves." While the thinking dispositions (reading, responding, and reflecting) are always present, facilitation moves are the public manifestations of those dispositions.

Some facilitation moves are predictable, and a facilitator may use them in every (or nearly every) protocol. Others are employed "on demand," drawn from the facilitator's repertoire as the occasion requires. Still others may be more impromptu, made up on the spot to address situations for which the facilitator does not have a ready-made move. And like moves on the basketball court, facilitation moves are not guaranteed to lead to their anticipated outcome. They sometimes result in consequences that require additional moves to keep the conversation on track.

While moves do not follow a set order, and certain moves may prove useful at any number of points in the conversation, we have parsed them into the three broad stages of a protocol in which they most often appear:

- *Getting a protocol (and each individual step of the protocol) started*
    Moves that set the stage
    Moves that set the tone

- *Moving through the protocol*
    Moves that set the pace
    Moves that encourage depth
    Moves for checking in with participants

- *Debriefing the protocol*
    Moves that invite reflection
    Moves that maintain focus on reflection
    Moves that support documenting the conversation

In many cases, the moves a facilitator makes can be accomplished through questions rather than directives, so many of the examples we use are phrased as such. Keep in mind, too, that these categories are porous: A single move may address two or more of these areas at the same time.

Of course, different protocols will require different moves. We do not provide tips for facilitating specific protocols, except as examples of moves that can be applied more generally. However, more specific tips can be very useful for the novice—or experienced—facilitator to review before facilitating one of the protocols. See *The Power of Protocols: An Educator's Guide to Better Practice* (McDonald et al., 2003) and *The Evidence Process: A Collaborative Approach to Understanding and Improving Teaching and Learning* (Evidence Project Staff, 2001) for protocol-specific tips.

This chapter does not provide a comprehensive catalog of moves and their uses (let alone all of their possible outcomes) but rather suggests some larger categories of moves facilitators use. The examples of specific moves we provide derive from our own facilitation as well as the many skilled facilitators we have had the good fortune to observe at work. Each facilitator will use moves in different ways, as well as develop her own moves, as part of the unique style with which she facilitates.

GETTING A PROTOCOL
(AND EACH INDIVIDUAL STEP OF THE PROTOCOL) STARTED

Facilitators often take time at the beginning of the protocol as a whole, and (more briefly) at the beginning of each new step, to orient the group to what the protocol asks for and why.

Moves That Set the Stage

Most facilitators have a set of tried-and-true moves with which they begin a protocol. These moves help the group understand the purpose for the conversation and the process by which they will work toward that purpose. But it would be a mistake to think that after beginning the protocol, the facilitator's responsibility for setting the stage is accomplished. While some stage-setting moves are used at the beginning of the conversation, others may be employed at strategic points along the way. In particular, the last two moves detailed here may help facilitators address possible gaps in understanding about the process that sometimes emerge during the conversation.

Reviewing the Purpose for the Protocol

It is easy to overlook purposes. Spending a few minutes on purpose at the beginning of a protocol can reduce the likelihood of confusion later on (although never entirely eliminate it):

- "Let's take a moment to remind ourselves of our reasons for doing this particular protocol."

If the protocol is one in a series of protocols that a group is undertaking in order to explore a particular issue about teaching and learning, the facilitator also might make time at the beginning of the conversation to review the highlights of previous protocols and name particular questions or insights that emerged in them.

Previewing the Steps of the Protocol

Groups usually benefit from having a good idea of the sequence of steps they'll be going through, as well as knowing something about what happens in each step. This brief preview can help participants gauge when to offer particular kinds of comments. This kind of move is particularly important when the group is using a new protocol or when new members have joined the group:

- "Let's walk through the steps of the protocol, and then see if anybody has questions before we begin."

Although it may be done very briefly, facilitators often preview the steps of a protocol even when the group is familiar with it.

Reminding the Group of the Presenter's Focusing Question

Some protocols allow the presenting teacher to name a focusing question (see Chapter 5) at the beginning of the conversation. While the presenting teacher normally introduces the focusing question as part of her presentation, the facilitator sometimes repeats it at the end of the presentation (giving the question emphasis) and reminds the group of the question at key points in the protocol. The facilitator also might write the question on chart paper or a board, making it visible throughout the conversation for the group to refer to.

Marking the Steps of the Protocol

At the beginning of each new step, facilitators typically remind participants of the purpose of that step and how it is enacted. In some cases, the facilitator provides an example of the kind of question or comment normally offered within this part of the conversation:

- "In this step, we are going to offer some feedback to the presenter. We'll try to offer feedback that addresses her focusing question. Feedback usually takes a couple of different forms, including . . ."

Making Distinctions

Protocols often require that participants make careful distinctions among various kinds of comments—for example, distinguishing between a clarifying question (which asks for specific, factual information) and a probing question (which invites the presenter or other participants to think more deeply about an issue). In protocols that make a distinction between descriptive comments and evaluative comments,

participants again may need further explanation to be able to distinguish between the two. To help participants make key distinctions,
facilitators can give direct explanations or invite group conversation
about them in the appropriate steps:

- "In this step, we want to focus only on clarifying questions,
  rather than on probing questions. Why don't we get a couple
  of examples of each and spend a few minutes talking about
  the difference?" (See Chapter 5 for further details about this
  distinction.)
- "It may be helpful as we enter into the feedback part of the
  protocol to review the distinction between 'criticism' and
  'critique.'" (See Chapter 8 for a discussion of this distinction.)
- "At this point in the protocol, we offer only descriptive comments. One way to know that you're pretty close to pure
  description is that you think most people in the room would
  see what you see and describe it the way you would."

The facilitator also might invite the group to practice descriptive comments, clarifying questions, or some other specific kind of participation as a warm-up exercise before the protocol begins.

Cueing the Presenter

Presenters sometimes need gentle reminders of their role in the protocol. Facilitators often anticipate and address some of the natural tendencies that may pull presenters away from their charge or task. For
example, if a protocol provides the presenter with a chance to respond
to the participants' conversation that occurred in the previous step, she
may need encouragement to steer away from defending or re-explain-
ing her work in favor of genuinely reflecting on the conversation and
identifying interesting ideas she heard in it:

- "Knowing that you will be digesting this over time, perhaps
  you could take 4 or 5 minutes now to just name some of the
  big ideas that you've heard and plan to think more about."

- "In responding to feedback, people tend to jump to the 'cool' comments, so be sure to address some of the 'warm' comments you heard as well."

Moves That Set the Tone

Setting the tone really begins even before the protocol opens (e.g., in how the facilitator invites the group to come to the table to get started). Setting "norms," the first move described below, may not be necessary before every protocol or in each of the group's meetings. A group that works together over time may set norms early in its work together and periodically revisit and review them. Typical norms include: "Be respectful of the work and the presenter," and "Monitor your own 'air time.'"

Like setting the stage, setting the tone can take on added importance when the group is in the thick of conversation—even if norms have been discussed earlier.

Developing a Set of Group Norms or Guidelines for the Conversation

In an early conversation with a group, the facilitator can invite participants to consider what will help them learn best in the conversation they're about to have. She then may lead the group in compiling a brief list of agreed-upon "group norms" to follow (or review and modify a list of norms previously developed):

- "What will help you learn best in this conversation?"
- "What norms or 'ground rules' have been present in other groups or meetings that you have been a part of that have helped make them good learning situations for you?"

Modeling and Referring to the Norms Throughout the Protocol

The facilitator should attempt to follow the norms and model them for the group in her conduct of the protocol. For example, if the norms call for "allowing time for reflection," the facilitator may try to build in extra periods for silent reflection or writing. Sometimes the facilitator might refer explicitly to the group norm she is attending to:

- "I can see from our list of norms that it might be good to give people a little more time to think before we jump into . . ."

Being Aware of Symbolic Behavior

While the behavior and comments of all group members influence the protocol, the facilitator's behavior is often more influential than that of other members of the group. Most group members look, consciously or not, to the facilitator for clues about how to participate in the conversation. For this reason, facilitators should be aware that little things they do or say may have a significant influence on the group.

The facilitator can use this influence in positive ways by, for example, asking a presenter's permission before entertaining certain kinds of questions or by inviting the group's input on a decision about next steps in the protocol:

- "How does the group feel about moving on to some 'cooler' feedback at this point?"

Other examples of symbolic behavior that can affect a protocol positively include calling on participants by name and thanking the individual participants who offer the first comments or questions in a new step of the protocol.

Symbolic behavior isn't limited to speech: Facilitators also model the seriousness and respectfulness of the enterprise in how they listen to a presenter or participant, how they look at samples of student or teacher work, by taking notes, and so on.

Making Space for Everybody to Be Heard and Participate

Protocols are much richer when they incorporate the perspectives of everybody in the group. However, we all know it is easier for some people than for others to enter a conversation. Facilitators encourage participation in many ways, from using a tone of voice that is welcoming to explicitly inviting participants who haven't spoken to contribute to the conversation:

- "Let's open the floor for clarifying questions."
- "Let's take a couple of minutes to invite anybody who hasn't spoken much to offer feedback."

Caution: Rarely, if ever, would a facilitator require somebody to speak. Some protocols call for "rounds" of participation (going in order around the circle), but in these it is normally permissible for participants to "pass" if they would rather not make a comment. Sometimes facilitators build in brief opportunities for participants to talk to a "neighbor" before inviting comments to be shared among the whole group. This provides an opportunity for everybody to be heard in a less public way.

MOVING THROUGH THE PROTOCOL

Introducing protocols and their various steps is an important role of the facilitator. Just as important are the moves a facilitator makes to keep the protocol engaging and productive once it is underway.

Moves That Set the Pace

Monitoring time is an important aspect of facilitation. Groups rarely have unlimited time for their protocols—most need to be conducted in an hour or less. Since groups usually need to complete all the steps of a protocol in one session, the facilitator is charged with keeping the conversation moving along. This often requires making a judgment call about whether to give more time to an emerging conversation in one part of the protocol or to move the group to the next part.

However, the goal of monitoring time is never to meet precisely the time guidelines provided in a protocol (these are always somewhat arbitrary, in any case, and some protocols don't even have them), but to use the time well for the group's purposes. Rather than think in terms of minutes, we suggest the facilitator think in terms of the group's pace: balancing comfort (i.e., not feeling rushed) with a tangible sense of moving ahead.

Timekeeping

Facilitators use different strategies for timekeeping. Some note on the printed protocol sheet the time they begin each phase of the conversation. This strategy may help keep the facilitator focused on her timekeeping responsibility and provide a rough idea of when it may be time to move on. Some facilitators may find it useful to ask a participant to monitor time and give the facilitator a signal when there is a minute or two left in the allotted time for a part of the conversation.

Practicing "Time Telling"

It is often helpful to let the group know how much time (roughly) it will have for a particular part of the protocol (or how much time is left once they're into it). This can help people think about their own participation in the conversation:

- "We've got just about 3 or 4 minutes left for feedback."

Moving On

Facilitators need to keep their eye on both the overall time the group has for the conversation—and how it is elapsing!—and the amount of time that is appropriate for each part of the conversation. There's no litmus test for when it is time to move on to the next step. Facilitators often ask for the group's input and then respond to it by either moving ahead or "earmarking" time for continuing the current part of the protocol:

- [*Responding to the group's input*] "Let's give just 5 more minutes/three or four more comments to this part of the conversation before moving ahead."
- "We've spent about 5 minutes on clarifying questions, and while there may be more we could ask, this may be a good time to move on to the next part of the protocol."

Finding a Segue

Facilitators look for natural "segues," such as particular comments or pauses, that may signal a natural shift in the conversation; but a facilitator cannot always count on these dropping into her lap. (The facilitator must balance this move with the value of "wait time"; see below.) Sometimes the clock dictates moving on, and the facilitator may need to arbitrarily—even unilaterally—advance the conversation:

- "I'm going to take advantage of this pause to suggest that we move on to the next step . . ."

Using Signs

Hand signals and other nonverbal cues help convey messages to participants. For example, the facilitator might hold up an open hand to indicate to the presenter or another participant that they are not supposed to speak at a particular point or that they have a minute or so to finish up. Even with such a system, the facilitator sometimes may need to interrupt verbally:

- "Excuse me, Lee, but at this point I think we are going to have to . . ."

Building in Time for Reflection

Some protocols include periods for reflection, for example, before offering feedback to the presenter. The facilitator, in reading the group, should look for those moments in the conversation when a minute or two of extra time for reflection might be productive:

- "Let's take a couple of minutes to organize our thoughts before we move on to . . ."

Being Comfortable with "Wait Time"

Even though the facilitator may feel like the clock is always ticking, adults need the same kind of wait time teachers provide for students after a question or prompt. Facilitators sometimes interpret silence as a signal that nobody has anything to say (and therefore that it is time to move on), rather than as an opportunity for reflection. More experienced facilitators demonstrate a greater comfort level with periods of silence (and even may come to enjoy them).

Moves That Encourage Depth

A facilitator has a tricky balance to maintain: She needs to make sure that the conversation is substantive, adheres to the parameters of the protocol, and addresses the problem or question framed by the presenter (or the group). However, she also needs to refrain from determining whether, for example, participants are making the right suggestions or are focusing on what she (the facilitator) deems to be the core issues raised by the work being discussed. The facilitator's work in a protocol is to make sure that the process has integrity as a collaborative inquiry or exploration, not to judge the value of the particular contributions being made by group members. The following moves aim at maintaining the integrity of the process.

Clarifying

As the facilitator reads her group during a protocol, she will discover there are many points when confusion or misunderstanding can occur. Participants and presenter can become confused about the purpose for the protocol, the presenter's focusing questions, what's being called for in a particular part of the protocol (e.g., the kinds of questions or feedback), and so on.

Of course, momentary confusion is natural in any conversation and very often will resolve itself as the conversation continues. Sometimes, however, an emerging misunderstanding or "fuzziness" might detract from the group's (or an individual participant's) ability to engage with the issues or the work on the table. In these cases, the facilitator may choose to intervene, typically by asking a question:

- "Would it help to take a look at what the protocol asks for in this part of the conversation?"
- "Is it clear what the presenter is asking for in the focusing question? Should we ask her to say a word about what leads her to ask this question?"
- "Which specific sample of work are you referring to? Can you point it out to us?"
- "I'm not sure I heard your question (or comment) correctly— could you repeat it, please?"

Modeling

The facilitator might choose to model a question, descriptive comment, evaluative comment, and so on, during the appropriate part of the protocol. Some facilitators choose to do this very transparently as they introduce and explain the purpose of a particular step:

- "A 'warm' comment might sound like, 'I really appreciate the way you've involved students in developing the rubric.'"

Facilitators also might choose to model less overtly: Recognizing that some participants may be confused about what a particular step calls for, a facilitator might decide to offer her own comment or question to give a clearer idea of what is expected.

Redirecting

Sometimes, a participant's contribution may come out of turn (e.g., offering evaluative feedback when the protocol calls for clarifying questions). This can put the facilitator in an awkward spot: If she singles out a participant's question or comment, suggesting it is somehow inappropriate, she may be seen as passing judgment on the participant. If, on the other hand, she lets it stand, this may trigger a series of such comments or questions, changing the nature of the conversation, or leading the presenter to become defensive (and thus less likely to listen and respond openly).

Rather than going down either of these paths, the facilitator may be able to redirect the comment or question, suggesting that the participant reintroduce it during a later period of the conversation:

- "Could you hang onto that comment until we get to the part of the protocol that calls for 'meatier' questions? It would fit well in the step in which we discuss implications for teaching and learning."
- "This question seems to suggest a particular point of view rather than a more neutral request for information. Why don't we save it for the open discussion portion of the protocol?"

The facilitator then may make a note to herself to remember to invite the participant to offer the redirected comment or question when the conversation gets to the appropriate point. However, she also may recognize that the participant may prefer not to be put on the spot, either because he might be sensitive to having the earlier episode reprised or because he might have reconsidered the appropriateness of the comment or question for any part of the conversation.

Asking for Evidence

One of the most natural tendencies in normal conversation is to offer perspectives and opinions, even in answering questions, without supporting what we say with specific evidence. In other words, many normal conversations rely on abstraction or generalization. Even teachers, with so much experience offering feedback to their students, often find it challenging in a professional learning conversation to support their comments on student work with concrete details. When they are able to do so, though, they often find that their ability to engage with the work (to "see" the work) and the group's ability to tackle important issues of teaching and learning related to it are enhanced. The questions facilitators use to ask for evidence often have the effect of inviting participants to reexamine their own questions or comments and the bases for forming them.

Since many conversations, in and out of school, tend to resist specificity and concreteness, a facilitator may feel awkward about asking for them, especially in the midst of the conversation. After all, it's one thing to say, "Let's try to be specific," at the beginning, and another to feel like one is pushing someone for evidence during the conversation. In our experience, the pushing is worth it: Participants, even those who may seem momentarily put off by being asked for evidence, are often appreciative of facilitators who exercise this move consistently. As in discussing a piece of art, identifying details, as well as overall impressions, opens up possibilities for the whole group to see the work with greater understanding and appreciate the complexities embedded in it.

Asking for evidence not only supports understanding but can deflect some rather unhelpful phenomena that can occur in learning conversations, including jumping to conclusions, dismissing possibilities based on a superficial reading, adopting a "quick-fix" approach to a problem (which rarely leads to real change), or going off track (e.g., into storytelling or "story-topping"). Two examples of questions facilitators ask are

- "What leads you to say that?"
- "Can you show us a place in the work where we'll see evidence of that?"

Encouraging Specificity

Specific questions, like specific comments, can help both the group and the presenter think more deeply about the work. Facilitators may ask participants to rephrase or refocus a question to make its intent more specific:

- "Can you focus that question on a specific aspect of the student work/assignment/teaching dilemma?"

Asking for Connections

A facilitator may ask a participant to identify a connection, for example, to the presenter's focusing question or to another participant's comment, in order to encourage greater focus or depth in the conversation:

- "Can you make a connection between your comment and the presenter's focusing question?"

Moves for Checking in with Participants

When the facilitator is not sure how to read the group or individual participants, asking participants directly about how they are experiencing the protocol is often the best way to go. There is a variety of ways facilitators go about this.

Taking a Facilitator's "Time Out"

Even facilitators can get lost or disoriented, especially in a learning conversation that is particularly intense or complex. It can benefit everybody for the facilitator to call "time out" and do some on-the-spot thinking with the group about the next step to take. In this kind of time out, the group might review the protocol guidelines, clarify the presenter's focusing question, discuss whether to spend more time than allotted on this part of the conversation, and so on:

- "I'd like to call a 'facilitator's time out' here so we can make a decision about . . ."

Taking the Group's "Temperature"

If a participant seems slightly lost or in some way put off by the conversation, the facilitator might check in briefly about the process with participants:

- "Let me just check to see if we're clear on the process for this part of the conversation. Does anybody have any questions or comments about the process at this point?"

Most facilitators normally avoid singling out an individual participant, even if she is obviously confused; but in groups that know each other well, a facilitator may feel comfortable doing so:

- "Colleen, it looks like you might have a question. Do you want to ask it now?"

DEBRIEFING THE PROTOCOL

Almost all protocols have a period at the end of the conversation in which participants step back from their examination and discussion of the student work, teacher work, or teaching dilemma, and instead focus on the process of the protocol itself. Facilitating reflection can be a tricky proposition since, by its nature, reflection may be unfocused, jumping from topic to topic. The facilitator tries to achieve a balance between creating an open space for all kinds of reflections, including a little "hopscotching," and keeping the group focused on addressing questions about the process that will be most beneficial to the group.

Moves That Invite Reflection

While some protocols name specific questions to be used, others leave it up to the facilitator to focus the debriefing. Some questions that might be used to prompt reflection include:

- "What about the protocol worked for you?"
- "What might have helped you or the group learn better?"
- "What could we try differently (or make sure we keep) the next time?"

Moves That Maintain Focus on Reflection

In practice, the facilitator often needs to counteract tendencies on the part of some participants to use the debrief step to ask the presenter one more question or to offer further advice or suggestions (those they didn't manage to get into the conversation earlier because of time constraints or parameters set by the protocol). It can be helpful to ask teachers to put away (or even turn over) the student work or teacher work that has been on the table in order to physically represent the mental shift from talking about the content (e.g., the student work) to talking about the process—how the protocol structure, facilitation, and so on supported a learning conversation.

Moves That Support Documenting the Conversation

Often, the debriefing period of the protocol can be a good time to ask for participants' help in capturing important moments in the conversation (recognizing, of course, that some important insights from a protocol don't reveal themselves for days, or even weeks, after the conversation has finished). Facilitators sometimes invite participants to share thoughts out loud to be captured on chart paper or sometimes ask participants to reflect by writing brief comments that can be read aloud (and might be collected as documentation of the group's progress). For example:

- "Why don't we each write down one moment in this protocol that really stands out for us and why?"
- "Thinking back over our past conversations, do you notice a theme or a series of questions that keep coming up? Perhaps everyone could write down one or two ideas and then we'll share some out loud."

AN EXAMPLE: MOVES IN THE CONTEXT OF A PROTOCOL

In this chapter we have outlined some categories and examples of moves that facilitators might choose to make during a protocol. To provide a clearer picture of how these moves work in the context of a specific protocol, we include below the steps of the Tuning Protocol, accompanied by our commentary of facilitating this protocol, including sample comments and questions that a facilitator might use in each of the steps. These additional remarks are not obligatory; we offer them simply as a resource for newer facilitators.

1. Introduction (5 minutes)

- Facilitator briefly introduces protocol goals, guidelines, and schedule.
- Participants briefly introduce themselves (if necessary).

Possible Facilitation Moves:

- "Before we get started, I'm going to briefly go over all the steps of the protocol so we know what we're getting into. At this point we are in the first step, the introduction; in a moment we'll move into the presentation during which . . ."
- [*If the group is new to protocols*] "Protocols sometimes can be a bit uncomfortable the first time through, so if you're feeling confused by the process, that's normal. You can ask me a question at any point, and we'll also have time to talk about the whole protocol process at the end of the protocol during the debriefing step."
- "Any questions before we get started?"

2. Presentation (10–15 minutes)

- The presenter has an opportunity to share the context for the student work, which might include information about the students and or/class, the assignment or prompt, learning goals (or standards) addressed, and evaluation methods used (rubric, scoring criteria, and so on).
- Presenting teacher frames a focusing question for feedback; facilitator may post focusing question for group to see.
- Participants are silent; no questions are entertained at this time.

Possible Facilitation Moves:

- [*If the focusing question doesn't come up*] "Did you want to say a few words about your focusing question and why it's important to you?"

3. Clarifying Questions (5 minutes)

- Participants ask "clarifying" questions in order to get information that may have been omitted in the presentation and that they feel would help them to understand the context for the student work. Clarifying questions are matters of "fact," easily answered by the presenter in a few words.
- The facilitator should be sure to limit the questions to those that are "clarifying," judging which questions more properly belong in the warm/cool feedback step.

Possible Facilitation Moves:

- "What's often tricky here is helping people ask actual clarifying questions rather than deeper, probing ones or questions that contain feedback or suggestions. Remember, these should be real 'nuts and bolts' kinds of questions, not deep, probing, 'What is the meaning of life?' questions. There will be time for those later during the warm and cool feedback step."
- [*To a participant who is asking a probing question*] "That might be a deeper question that gets into values or beliefs. Can you hang onto it for the warm and cool feedback step of the protocol?"
- [*To a participant whom you think is asking a probing question*] "I'm going to make a 'facilitator's call' here and suggest that that's deeper than a clarifying question. Hang onto it for the warm and cool feedback step of the protocol."
- [*To the presenting teacher, if you are not certain whether a question is clarifying or probing*] "Can you answer that very briefly and concretely? Otherwise, let's take it up in warm and cool feedback."

4. Examination of Student Work Samples (10–15 minutes)

- Participants look closely at the work, keeping the presenter's focusing question in mind, perhaps taking notes for the warm and cool feedback.

- Presenter is silent; participants do this work silently or talk quietly with a neighbor.

Possible Facilitation Moves:

- [*At the beginning of this step*] "During this part of the protocol, the focus is on the student work. It's not a time to ask the presenting teacher questions or engage in conversation with her. It's fine to talk quietly about the work with a neighbor. It might even help you to get clearer about the feedback you want to offer."
- [*To the presenting teacher*] "Any quick thing you need to say to us about the work before we get started looking at it?"

5. Pause to Reflect on Warm and Cool Feedback (2–3 minutes)

- Participants take a few minutes to reflect individually on what they would like to contribute to the feedback session.
- Presenter is silent.

Possible Facilitation Moves:

- [*To introduce this step*] "As you finish up looking at the student work, take a couple minutes to identify some warm and cool feedback you'd like to offer the presenting teacher. Warm feedback points out strengths in the student work or the instructional context for it. Cool feedback points to possible gaps or weaknesses and often comes in the form of a question. As much as possible, try to connect your feedback to the focusing question we heard during the presentation. It's also very helpful to be as specific as possible with your feedback and point to places in the work that led you to offer it."

6. Warm and Cool Feedback (10–15 minutes)

- Participants share feedback with one another while the presenter listens. The feedback typically begins with a few minutes of warm feedback, moves on to a few minutes of cool feedback, and then to a mix of the two.

- *Warm feedback* points to strengths, for example, comments about how the work presented seems to meet the desired goals. *Cool feedback* identifies possible "disconnects," or gaps, between the work and the teacher's goals for it; cool feedback is often phrased as a question.
- The facilitator may need to remind participants of the presenter's focusing question.
- Presenter is silent; he or she may choose to take notes.

Possible Facilitation Moves:

- [*To the group*] "Rather than go around in a strict order, I suggest people speak when they feel comfortable. It's okay not to speak—no one should feel they *have* to say something. Let's start by getting some warm feedback on the table. Who'd like to begin?"
- [*To the presenter*] "I'm going to ask the participants to direct their comments toward each other rather than toward you. You might want to push your chair back from the table a bit, so you can be more like a fly on the wall, listening in on a conversation about your work. This approach generally takes a bit of the pressure off the presenter—she won't feel as much urge to jump into the conversation as the group talks."
- It's nice to thank the first few people who offer feedback.
- [*If a comment seems a little vague or general*] "Is there something specific in the student work or other materials you could point to that made you say that?"
- You don't want to ask a follow-up question after all or even most comments. That would make the protocol too facilitator-centric.
- "We've had a good range of warm feedback to this point. Can we start to identify some cool feedback? That doesn't mean we need to give up on the warm, just mix in some cooler feedback, too."
- [*To a participant who's starting to give a whole list of comments*] "Thanks, Darryl. Let's get some other perspectives on the table."
- [*If, after a time, no one seems to be directly addressing the presenter's focusing question*] "Let's keep the focusing question in

mind. [*Repeat it for the group.*] Does anyone want to speak directly to this question?"

- [*To a participant*] "In your own mind, do you connect that comment to the presenting teacher's focusing question? How so?"

7. Reflection (5–10 minutes)

- Presenter addresses those comments/questions s/he chooses to. The purpose is not to defend the student work or his/her work, but instead to reflect aloud on those ideas or questions that seemed particularly compelling or intriguing.
- Facilitator may intervene to help focus, clarify, and so on.
- Participants listen silently.

Possible Facilitation Moves:

- [*To the presenting teacher before she speaks*] "Before we turn the floor over to you, I just want to remind you and all of us that the goal here is for you to reflect or think out loud about some of the things you heard that caught your attention. It's not your job to answer all of our questions or speak to all of our comments. In fact, I'd suggest you pick out just a couple of areas that were most provocative to your thinking and talk about those."
- [*To the presenter if she does not address the focusing question*] "Did you want to say anything about what you heard that got at your focusing question?"

8. Debrief (5–10 minutes)

- Facilitator leads discussion focused on the process, rather than content, of the discussion (i.e., how the protocol supported a learning conversation).
- Everyone participates.

Possible Facilitation Moves:

- "Before we debrief the protocol, let's thank the presenting teacher for what she just did for all of us by putting her work and her students' work on the table."

- "In this part of the protocol, we are turning our attention away from the student work and the presenter's focusing question to just focus on the process of conversation and this Tuning Protocol structure. As a symbol of this shift in our conversation, why don't we put away the copies of student work?"
- "Why don't we start with the presenting teacher and hear about her experience of the protocol, then let others into the conversation: What did it feel like? What worked for you? What questions or concerns does it raise? Of course, you can just say 'pass.'"
- "Okay, let's hear others address those questions from their perspectives as participants."
- Sometimes the temptation as the facilitator is to try to answer questions or concerns about the process as they come up. It's usually best to let a range of comments or questions get named, then spend some time talking as a group about the ones that seem most significant to the group.

Again, this list of moves is not intended to be a script for facilitating the Tuning Protocol but rather an example of how moves might be contextualized in particular steps. Situations will arise in a Tuning Protocol that call for other kinds of moves; conversely, many of these moves may be useful in protocols quite different from the Tuning Protocol. Practice and reflection are the best ways of developing a personal repertoire of moves that work best for a facilitator and for the group she facilitates.

SUMMING UP

No single move is guaranteed to produce exactly the results that the facilitator hopes it will. Probably every facilitator knows the feeling of regretting having made a particular move (instead of a different one or no move at all). Fortunately, individual moves are rarely if ever fatal to the conversation. While it is true that, as Tom Waits sings, "you can't unring a bell," it may be possible to undo a move. A different move may help right the conversation; and often the conversation will right itself without any other intervention. Conversations supported by protocols should be safe places for everybody, the facilitator included, to make mistakes and learn from them.

Chapter 5

What Kinds of Questions Get Asked in a Protocol?

As the title of this book suggests, questions play an important role in facilitating protocols. However, asking questions in a protocol is by no means limited to the facilitator. In fact, one of the facilitator's most significant responsibilities is to encourage participants to ask questions of different kinds during the protocol.

As discussed in the previous chapter, facilitators employ a range of moves to encourage substantive conversation, or "depth," within a protocol. Many of these moves involve helping participants adhere closely to the protocol and its parameters, with the recognition that it is often the rigorous discipline of a protocol-guided conversation that nurtures depth. Thus, the fine distinctions that participants are asked to make among different categories of questions are not "semantic antics" (however much it might seem so to the novice participant!) but a powerful step toward generating a thought-provoking conversation.

Beyond recognizing categories of questions, participants need to develop the ability to distinguish between more and less effective questions within each of those categories. In order to help participants develop effective questions of various kinds, the facilitator herself needs to understand—and be able to communicate—the distinctions and qualities that are the hallmarks of powerful and appropriate questions in a protocol. This chapter considers the three kinds of questions that appear most frequently in protocols: (1) focusing questions, (2) clarifying questions, and (3) probing questions.

Note: This chapter draws extensively on materials developed by the National School Reform Faculty (NSRF) and especially on the work of Gene Thompson-Grove, Faith Dunne, and Edorah Fraser. The NSRF is a professional development initiative that focuses on developing collegial relationships, encouraging reflective practice, and rethinking leadership in restructuring schools—all in support of increased student achievement. For more information about NSRF, see *www.nsrfharmony.org*.

FOCUSING QUESTIONS

A focusing question is a question developed by the presenting teacher. The question usually captures the essence of why she is bringing the work to the group and what she hopes to learn from the group's discussion. The focusing question is unique among question types in that it typically is developed before the protocol and guides the selection of materials (including student and teacher work samples) that will be presented in the protocol (see Chapter 6).

In some protocols (the Tuning Protocol, the Consultancy), the presenting teacher articulates her focusing question for the group as part of her presentation. In other protocols (the Collaborative Assessment Conference, for example), the presenting teacher does not have to present a focusing question to the group. Even in these kinds of protocols, however, the presenting teacher still needs to give careful thought to why she has chosen to share the particular work that she wants to share and why she thinks group discussion of that work will be helpful. Although the question is not shared with the group initially in such situations, clarity about her own questions and puzzles can guide the presenter in selecting appropriate work to present and help her sift through the many different kinds of comments that will emerge as she listens to participants discussing the work.

Qualities of a Good Focusing Question

While focusing questions vary widely in their content, good ones typically have a few features in common:

- *Importance.* They capture an issue or puzzle that the presenter cares about deeply and sees as central to her practice—an issue she has wrestled with and about which she genuinely seeks other perspectives to help her make progress.
- *Relevance.* They focus on an issue that has relevance and interest for other educators. The issue is one that can be discussed productively by a group of colleagues, and colleagues as well as the presenter are likely to learn something from the discussion.
- *A close connection to student learning.* The issue bears on student learning in a fairly direct way.

In this section, we offer some examples of the kinds of focusing questions that are typical for various protocols, as well as some ideas about the kinds of materials the presenter might bring to help participants engage effectively with her question.

Examples of Focusing Questions for a Tuning Protocol

Focusing questions in a Tuning Protocol typically invite feedback on specific issues that the presenting teacher wants to revise and improve: an assignment, an assessment tool, a unit of instruction, specific learning goals, and so on. Most of the questions in a Tuning Protocol are asked in relation to student work. For example

- "How can I support students in developing and demonstrating their research skills through this project?"
- "How can my rubric give students more feedback to support their revision of . . . ?"
- "How well does the assessment tool (e.g., rubric) I use match the learning goals I have for the assignment? How could it be improved?"
- "In what ways does this student work meet (or fail to meet) this particular state standard?"

Typically, presenting teachers in a Tuning Protocol bring a variety of materials to share with colleagues: copies of the assignment, the learning goals, the assessment tools (a rubric, scoring criteria), and so on. She also brings samples of work from several students (typically three to five students, representing a range of levels of work).

Examples of Focusing Questions for the Consultancy

The Consultancy focuses on a dilemma that has no easy solution. Here are some typical focusing questions in a Consultancy (we also have included just a bit of the context the presenting teacher would normally provide):

- "No matter how hard I try to be inclusive and ask for [colleagues'] ideas, about half of the people don't want to do anything new—they think things were just fine before. How do I work with the people who don't want to change without alienating them?"

- "I know that creative project work keeps my students engaged and eager to learn, but those kinds of projects take so long to carry out, and we have so much material to cover to satisfy the state-mandated tests. How can I serve both the goals of the tests and my own goal of keeping students engaged and involved?"

Often, presenters in the Consultancy write out their dilemma along with their focusing question. (Oral presentations of the dilemma are also possible.) The presenter also may choose to bring samples of student work or her own work to share with the group in order illustrate the dilemma, but the dilemma and the focusing question (not the work samples) serve as the focus of the discussion.

Examples of (Focusing) Questions for a Collaborative Assessment Conference

As noted earlier, the Collaborative Assessment Conference does not require the presenter to share a focusing question with the group (although in the step toward the end of the protocol in which the presenter provides some context, she is welcome to share her questions, if she chooses), so the presenter's question does not "focus" the group discussion as it does in other protocols. Nevertheless, presenters do bring with them questions about the work they are sharing. The kinds of questions that lead teachers to present work in a Collaborative Assessment Conference often have a "puzzling" or "wondering" quality to them:

- "This particular piece of student work puzzles and intrigues me. Why did the student do it this way? How would others interpret or make sense of this work?"
- "This is work from a student I never seem to be able to reach: What insights might I be able to gain from a group conversation about who this student is and how I might work more effectively with him or her?"

Presenters in the Collaborative Assessment Conference often bring a single piece of student work—or sometimes several pieces from the same student. Very occasionally, work from multiple students is examined. The presenter might want to bring additional supporting materials (assignment sheets, and so on) to hand out during her response time (after the group has discussed the work), but additional artifacts beyond the student work usually are not necessary.

CLARIFYING QUESTIONS

Clarifying questions are simple questions of fact. Clarifying questions typically play a key role in protocols, such as the Tuning Protocol or the Consultancy, in which the presenting teacher makes an initial presentation to the group that provides the context of the work before the group members examine and discuss that work. The step inviting participants to ask "clarifying questions" usually comes shortly after the presentation. The goal of clarifying questions is to clarify the presentation and provide the "nuts and bolts" information that participants need in order to ask good probing questions and provide useful feedback later in the protocol.

Participants ask clarifying questions primarily to enhance their own (not the presenter's) understanding. Clarifying questions have brief, factual answers and don't seek to provide any new "food for thought" for the presenter. Typically, they should not go beyond the boundaries of the particular project or dilemma that the presenting teacher has shared. The litmus test for a clarifying question is: Does the presenter have to think much (or deeply) before s/he answers? If so, it's almost certainly a probing question.

Here are some examples of clarifying questions:

- "How much time did the project take?"
- "How were the students grouped?"
- "What resources did the students have available for this project?"

Sometimes it is difficult to distinguish between a clarifying question and a more substantive or "probing" question (see below); for example, "How was the student work assessed?" If the question can be answered briefly and factually, it can be treated as a clarifying question and answered immediately; if it requires more reflection or a more elaborate response from the presenting teacher, it probably should be treated as a probing question or as feedback and be "redirected" to later in the protocol (see Chapter 4).

PROBING QUESTIONS

The Consultancy invites the participants to ask probing questions. Probing questions are also an especially good kind of feedback within a Tuning Protocol and similar protocols, although (unlike in the Consultancy) the presenting teacher does not answer them immediately or, necessarily, at all. In contrast to clarifying questions, probing questions are intended to help the presenter think more deeply about the issue at hand. The presenter often doesn't have a ready answer to a genuine probing question. In addition, good probing questions

- are open-ended (rather than yes/no), allowing for multiple responses
- elicit a slower or more considered response
- move thinking from reaction to reflection
- encourage taking a different perspective
- help create a "paradigm shift" in the presenting teacher's (and, possibly, the group's) thinking
- assist the presenter to explore and address her own question/dilemma (rather than deferring to someone with greater or different expertise)
- may be general and widely applicable
- don't place blame on anyone
- are usually brief (although weighty)

Tips for Crafting Probing Questions

Participants in a protocol can find it challenging to come up with good probing questions. The following guidelines (framed as questions from the participant's perspective) can help:

- "Do I have a 'right' answer in mind?" (If so, the participant should either revise the question so that it is more open-ended or not ask it.)

- "Is my question relevant to the presenter's focusing question, or am I pursuing my own agenda?"
- "Does my question encourage the presenter to take a risk without making her feel threatened or accused?"
- "Does my tone make it clear that I am advocating for the presenter's success?"

Distinguishing Between Probing Questions and Recommendations

Often, what a participant thinks is a probing question is actually a recommendation in disguise. If she finds herself asking questions that begin, "Have you thought of doing . . . ?" or, "Why don't you try . . . ?" she probably has strayed into the territory of recommendations. While recommendations are valuable and often are given a particular place in protocols, they usually do not serve the purpose of helping the presenter look at her issue or question in a new light—the ultimate goal of a good probing question.

With a little thought and effort—and "cueing" from the facilitator—recommendations can be turned into probing questions. Consider this example from an actual Consultancy. The presenting teacher, a math instructor, was trying to figure out why the strongest math students in the class weren't buying in and doing their best work on what seemed to be interesting math "problems of the week." Participants offered the following responses during the "probing questions" step:

- "You could have students use the rubric to assess their own papers." (recommendation)
- "Could you have the students use the rubric to assess their own papers?" (recommendation restated as a question)
- "What would happen if students used the rubric to assess their own work?" (recommendation restated as a probing question)
- "What do the students think is an interesting math problem?" (good probing question)
- "What would have to change for students to work more for themselves and less for you?" (better probing question)

Examples of Probing Questions

The following questions and question stems may be useful for developing probing questions:

- "Why do you think this is the case?"
- "Why is this such a dilemma for you?"
- "What would have to change in order for . . . ?"
- "What do you wish . . . ?"
- "What's another way you might . . . ?"
- "What might you see happening in your classroom if . . . ?"
- "How was...different from . . . ?"
- "What is the connection between . . . and . . . ?"
- "What sort of an impact do you think . . . ?"
- "How did you decide/determine/conclude . . . ?"
- "What was your intention when . . . ?"
- "What do you assume to be true about . . . ? What if the opposite were true? Then what?"
- "How might your assumptions about . . . have influenced how you are thinking about . . . ?"
- "Why . . . ?" "Why . . . ?" "Why . . . ?" (Sometimes several "why" questions, asked in succession, can be very effective.)

Here are some full-blown probing questions:

- "Why is this approach the best way to introduce this concept?"
- "How do you think your own relationship to the material has influenced your choice of instructional strategies?"
- "What do the students think is quality work? A challenging task?"
- "What would the students involved say about this issue?"
- "Why do you think the team is struggling with interdisciplinary curriculum planning?"
- "What would understanding of this mathematical concept look like? How would you know students have 'gotten it'?"
- "What evidence do you have from this student's work that her ability to reach substantiated conclusions has improved?"
- "How do you think your expectations for students might have influenced their work on this project?"

- "What do you think would happen if you restated your professional goals as questions?"
- "What other approaches have you considered for helping students to understand this concept?"

*   *   *

As we have seen, distinctions among different types of questions can be
slippery. What may seem clear in reading about questions or in framing a focusing question during a preconference with the presenting
teacher (see Chapter 6) may become foggy in the midst of the protocol
itself. Chapter 4 offers some moves that a facilitator can make to "check
in" with participants about their understanding of the process, for
example, asking, "What kind of questions does the protocol ask for
here?" or, "What do we mean by 'clarifying questions' anyway?" Before
getting into the protocol itself, it can be beneficial, especially in more
novice groups, to discuss different types of questions a protocol typically calls for and to practice asking a few of each (perhaps using the
guidelines and examples in this chapter).

Just as time, practice, and reflection help people become better
questioners in their teaching, so they enable participants in protocols
to develop and ask questions that move the conversation forward and
deepen the learning for everyone in the group.

Chapter 6

What Happens
Before and After Protocols?

A protocol-guided conversation about student or teacher work (or both) is usually the most visible—and public—part of a larger process of discussion, deliberation, preparation, and reflection that begins before the group meets and continues after it adjourns. In this chapter, we focus on some of the things the facilitator does before and after meetings to help the group achieve its purposes. We begin by considering three major tasks facilitators take on in preparing for a meeting at which one or more protocols will take place: (1) planning the agenda, (2) communicating with the group, and (3) working with the teacher(s) who will be presenting work in the protocol(s).

In discussing the third task, we describe several critical elements of the presenting teacher's preparation: framing a question or problem about the work she is presenting, selecting materials (student and/or teacher work samples and/or a description of a problem or dilemma) to present, and choosing an appropriate protocol. The facilitator often helps the presenter frame her question, select materials, and choose a protocol in a more or less formal "preconference." (The choice of protocols, a decision in which the facilitator is instrumental, is discussed more fully in Chapter 7.)

Finally, we consider how facilitators work with groups after a protocol to encourage the presenter and participants to reflect on what they are learning, as well as identifying new questions for exploration or inquiry.

BEFORE THE MEETING

In Chapter 3, we introduced three domains of facilitation: facilitating learning, logistics, and longevity. Preparing for a meeting in which protocols will be used requires attention to both learning and logistics. First we will focus on the more logistical pieces (creating an agenda and communicating with the group) that create a platform for learning, and then the more learning-centered element (although one that still involves logistical considerations) of working with the presenter.

Creating an Agenda

Everybody probably knows what it feels like to come to a meeting in which no one seems to have thought about how the group will use the time to achieve its goals. The experience can be enervating, even exasperating. By contrast, when a facilitator has given thoughtful attention to the group goals and the structure of the meeting, the facilitator's efforts can be nearly invisible: The group may not even notice her careful planning because they are so engaged in the very learning that the structure has facilitated.

Designing such a structure takes work and ranks among the facilitator's most important tasks (in addition to finding a time and place to meet, of course!). While some people think the protocol itself provides the meeting agenda, in fact, protocols usually are not the only things that happen when a group convenes to discuss student or teacher work. (See Figure 6.1 for a sample meeting agenda.)

We know of no secret for creating the perfect agenda, but we can share some things we have learned and try to keep in mind as we think about how time (usually in short supply) may be used productively.

Figure 6.1. Sample Agenda for Meeting at Which Protocols Will Take Place

---

Looking at Sudent Work Meeting
October 12

Agenda:

1. Catch up and review the agenda
2. Reflect on the last meeting
3. Tuning Protocol (Marci presents)
4. Modified Collaborative Assessment Conference Protocol (Jim presents)
5. Plan for next meeting

- *Get input from the group.* At the end of a meeting or in between meetings, the facilitator may ask the group to suggest items for the next meeting's agenda. Collaboratively structured agendas generally contribute to all participants' sense of investment in the meeting.
- *Balance ambition and reality.* In putting together agendas, facilitators must check the impulse to try to do too much, even as they strive to use the time they have to the fullest. With experience, facilitators get a feel for how much time to allocate to different agenda items, for example, "We usually can do one long protocol and two shorter ones."
- *Allow for some "breathing room."* Protocols require intense concentration. Meetings may benefit from less structured time at the start of a meeting for the group to get settled and share news before getting down to work. Similarly, a bit of time for more casual exchanges in between protocols or at the end of the meeting also can be helpful.
- *Write the agenda down and share it with the group.* While groups certainly can meet productively without a written agenda, making the agenda explicit and visible gives the group a map of where it is going and decreases the likelihood of unproductive side trips. Agendas need not be elaborate: A brief list of key items (like the one in Figure 6.1) is fine. Jotting brief notes about the meeting on the agenda sheet and then saving the sheet can provide an easy, useful form of documentation of a group's work.
- *Review the agenda at the start of the meeting.* This usually gets the group in gear and allows for some last-minute adjustments (additions, switching the order around, and so on).
- *Be flexible and responsive.* As Gene Thompson-Grove of the National School Reform Faculty says, "All agendas are either tentative or historical." Facilitators expect agendas to change in response to what happens during the meeting. This should not be taken as an excuse to depart from the agenda without some deliberation. Knowing when to help the group move forward with the original plan and when to reevaluate the agenda always requires the facilitator to "read" the group. If

the facilitator does decide to alter the agenda, she needs to make the change clear and explicit for the group, thereby helping them understand the meeting's direction and enabling them to share responsibility for the process.

- *Keep notes.* Try to record the emerging questions, issues, or ideas that the group does not have time to explore in the meeting but that could be taken up in future meetings.

A reality check: Sometimes, no matter how well crafted the agenda, real life throws a curve: The presenting teacher is out, or the student work that she had planned to present didn't happen, and so on. Rather than cancel meetings, groups can do some collaborative problem solving. For example, a teacher may grab some student work that is near at hand, and the group can decide on a productive way to talk about it. Or the group might choose to take up an issue that has surfaced in previous protocols and that it has not yet had time to explore fully. One thing can always be said about schools: There is never a shortage of important things to work on or talk about.

Communicating with the Group (and Others)

A big part of what the facilitator does before and after the group's meetings involves communication. Schools can be frenetic places as teachers and administrators try to accomplish so much with so many students in so little time. Maintaining clear, ongoing, and supportive communication in such a setting is as challenging as it is crucial.

While working with the presenter is, arguably, the most critical aspect of premeeting communication (and will be treated in the next section), the facilitator needs to check in with anybody who may be playing a role in the meeting, for example, a participant who might facilitate one of the protocols or act as recorder or bring snacks. Often there will be other items on the agenda to consider besides protocols. For example, if a member of the group is making a presentation or leading part of the meeting, she will need to know how much time she has and how her piece works with the other parts of the meeting.

Even if other group members are not playing "marquee roles," the facilitator might communicate with them as well, via e-mail, phone, or memo a day or two before the meeting. The reminder message might include the time and place of the meeting as well as a brief preview of the agenda and what the group will be working on. The principal also needs to be in the communication loop. Like the members of the group, she needs to know when and where the meeting is, who is participating, and what is on the agenda. One reason to stay in touch with the administration is to anticipate logistical issues that could become problems (scheduling, space, coverage for teachers, and so on). If there is an outside partner (such as a school coach) involved in the meetings on a regular or an occasional basis, the facilitator usually touches base with her about what the group has planned, who is playing a role in the meeting, and so on.

Sometimes the facilitator may feel a bit like a parent, seemingly telling people the same things over and over; however, with school calendars so crowded and teachers' days so full, people usually appreciate the reminders.

Working with the Presenting Teacher

Before a teacher presents her own work, samples of her students' work, or a dilemma or problem from her classroom, she engages in a deliberate process of selecting materials, framing a question or problem, choosing a protocol, and putting the presentation together. The presenting teacher has two critical decisions to make. First, what question or problem will she frame for herself and/or the group to promote a discussion that is engaging and useful? (While some protocols such as the Collaborative Assessment Conference do not require the presenting teacher to name this question or problem for the group, it is still important for her to be clear about her own motivation for sharing the work and what she hopes to learn from the conversation.) Second, how will she select materials (e.g., student and teacher work samples) that support that discussion? The facilitator typically works with the presenter on addressing both these questions.

Although we are discussing the issue of framing a question before we turn to selecting materials, there is no set order in which to address these questions. In fact, as we discuss later in the chapter, the presenter usually moves back and forth frequently between these two elements, making adjustments to both, before she is satisfied with how she will frame her problem and what work she will present to the group.

Framing a Question or Problem

One critical element in preparing to present is thinking about how the group will look at the work, with what goals, and with what intended (although not guaranteed) outcomes—for the presenter and the group. While such framing is the prerogative of the presenter, the facilitator can offer valuable support through asking questions that help the presenter articulate, for herself and eventually for the group, goals for looking at the work.

Two overarching questions that guide framing a protocol, as articulated by Steve Seidel of Project Zero, are: "What do you want to learn?" and "Why are we doing this as a group?" Some questions that follow from these, which facilitators may ask to stimulate a presenter's thinking about her goals, include

- "What do you want help with?" (e.g., an assignment that didn't go well, developing an assessment tool)
- "What's puzzling or intriguing you?" (e.g., students' responses to a prompt, differences in skill levels, or approaches to solving a problem)
- "What's keeping you up at night?" (e.g., concerns about a particular student, a teaching dilemma)

Of course, a presenter's group (or the presenter herself) may already have identified questions that will help guide the selection of materials; for example, "How can we help students develop research skills?" or, "How well is our recently adopted reading program working?" The facilitator may help the presenter "customize" the group's question in light of the presenter's own students and her particular interests or concerns. Once a question or interest emerges, the facilitator and presenter can "fine-tune" it by considering how it might be posed to the group as a "focusing question."

Not all protocols require the presenter to name an explicit focusing question. However, even if the presenter ultimately chooses a protocol that does not call for one (e.g., the Collaborative Assessment Conference), she and the facilitator should talk over her reasons for wanting to present a particular piece of work: What are her implicit questions? What does she hope to learn from the group's conversation? (In Chapter 5, we provide some guidelines for and examples of different kinds of focusing questions typical of different protocols.)

Selecting Materials to Present

If one thinks about all the student work, teacher work, and day-to-day teaching dilemmas to which the typical classroom gives rise, one might conclude that the possibilities for work to share in a protocol are virtually limitless. Unless it is random, selection therefore must be guided by some controlling idea or impulse. If the presenter has framed her question or puzzle as discussed above, that certainly will help guide selection. On the other hand, a less well-defined interest or concern—for example, an individual student who is puzzling to the teacher, a recent task or project that didn't go quite as the teacher expected, or a teaching strategy that she has been working on—can provide a starting point for the presenter's selection and, eventually, more explicit framing.

At this point in the preparation, a facilitator may ask: "In order to get at your interest in . . . , what would be the most useful work to present?" As a resource, Figure 6.2 provides a partial listing of possibilities grouped into three categories.

Figure 6.2. Work Selection "Menu"

Student Work Samples	Teacher Work Samples	Other Data
• Single samples of work from individual students	• Unit plan	• Self- or peer-assessment instrument
	• Lesson plan	
	• Activity or project plan	• Observations (by teacher, peer, other observer)
• Multiple samples over time by individual students	• Assessment instrument (rubric, checklist)	
		• Documentation of classroom activity (photos, video, audio)
• Samples from multiple students from the same assignment		
		• Teacher's reflections (reflective writing, journals, e-mail to facilitator, and so on)
• Work in different stages (drafts) from an individual student		
		• Student reflections (written or oral)
• Work in different stages (drafts) from multiple students		

As with the proverbial menu from a Chinese restaurant, it is often useful to choose "one from column A and one from column B," for example, the teacher's assignment and samples of student work carried out in response to it; or a sample of student work along with students' reflections on the original project to which they were responding. Giving participants different kinds of materials, when those materials are genuinely related, often strengthens protocols.

The menu may be a useful starting place, but it leaves many more-nuanced selection problems for the presenter to work out. For example, deciding on samples of work from multiple students invites the questions, "How many students' work?" and, "Which students' work?" Facilitators may be able to offer advice by drawing on their experience in other protocols or using other resources, such as the chart for matching protocols to purposes, presented in Chapter 7 (see Figure 7.1).

The presenter and the facilitator often talk through the pieces the presenter might bring, given her framing interest or question. Rather than evaluating the possibilities ("that sounds good"), facilitators can be most helpful by asking questions that help clarify decisions for the presenter; for example, "What are the advantages of presenting this piece (rather than others)?" or, "Are there other pieces (or additional pieces) that might allow participants to better address your question?"

Facilitators also can be helpful in relieving presenters of some of the anxiety that may build up around preparing for a protocol. Selecting student or teacher work to present is not an exact science. Even if the pieces selected turn out to be poorly suited to the presenter's question or the group's purpose, the conversation still may prove productive. As discussed in Chapter 1, the focusing question and the student work presented are just two of the points of influence on a protocol.

Choosing and Reviewing a Protocol

Selecting a protocol is often the area in which the facilitator's help is most needed during the preparation period. Discussing protocols can be useful at any stage of the framing and selecting process, although it is important to remember that framing and selecting should influence the choice of protocol, not be ruled by it (unless, for some reason, the group has decided it wants to try out or practice a particular protocol). In Chapter 7, we look more closely at the issues of matching purpose to protocol.

When the facilitator and presenter (and/or the group) have chosen a protocol, the facilitator usually reviews the steps with the presenter to ensure the presenter knows what is expected of her and the group, the order of the steps, and approximately how much time each will take. For example, the presenter needs to know that at a certain point in a Tuning Protocol, she will listen to some "cool" (as well as "warm") feedback, or that in a Collaborative Assessment Conference, she won't be able to give any context about the student work she presents until after the participants have examined and discussed the work.

The Preconference

A facilitator typically assists the presenter in preparing for her presentation in a one-on-one meeting before the protocol, sometimes referred to as a preconference. The preconference can be a regular part of the group's work, for example, a conversation held a week before the group's regular meeting in which the presenter and the facilitator go through a number of preparation activities. With more experienced participants, the preconference often is handled more informally, as a check-in conversation (over the phone, during a free period, or "on the fly").

It is not always possible, or necessary, to have a preconference before the meeting itself. In groups that are comfortable working with protocols, some of what happens in a preconference can be built into the group's meeting time: Presenting teachers bring the work they have selected and their framing questions (or concerns) to the meeting, and the facilitator asks which protocol would be most useful and appropriate. The decision about which protocol to use is then made with input from the group.

The preconference involves all of the questions we have discussed previously about selection and framing, and often involves moving back-and-forth between those two concerns. For example, for a presenter who has a strong idea of the work she would like to present, the facilitator might raise questions about why this particular material is interesting to her, what the presenter hopes to learn, and so on, gradually moving from selection to framing. Often, once a presenter develops a clearer frame, she refines her initial selection of material.

Conversely, a presenter may have a pretty good idea of her question but feel less clear on what pieces of work will help her and the group address her question. (Sometimes this comes about when the question is determined by the group.) In this case, the facilitator might ask questions that help the presenter explore the range of materials she could present: "What work have your students done that you might want to share? What aspects of your own work could the group discuss? What other kinds of materials might be useful?" Eventually, the facilitator can ask questions that help narrow the scope ("Which particular pieces?" "From which assignment?" "Which students?" "What format?" "How could you capture that?" and so on).

Preparation may take more than one preconference. Sometimes an initial conversation raising some of the questions about framing and selecting may be followed up with another conversation, once the presenter has a better idea of the question she wants to frame and the work she wants to present in her protocol.

Preparing the Presentation

With the questions framed, materials selected, and protocol chosen, the presenter still needs to think about how she will share the context of her work with the group. Some protocols call for the presenter to open the session with an initial presentation about the work and its context. In other protocols, the presentation of context and issues comes later in the structure. Either way, the presenter needs to give some thought to what she will say to the group about the materials she is sharing and why she is sharing them.

The goal of putting together the presentation in advance is not to rehearse a polished production but to think about how the form and content of the presentation serve the presenter's and the group's learning goals. Some questions facilitators may ask to help presenters in preparing include:

- *For a protocol in which the presenter gives initial context information*: How much context will the group need to be able to look at the work in an informed way? How can you provide that in just a few minutes?

- *For a protocol in which the context is shared after the work has been examined and discussed*: What aspects of the context for the work seem most significant to you? How can you relate that context in just a few minutes? Are there other materials that you might want to share after the student (or teacher) work has been discussed?
- *For protocols in which the presenter provides an initial focusing question*: Would it be useful to write out your focusing question on chart paper to keep it visible and present in participants' thinking? (Facilitators often help the presenter refine the wording of her issue or question so that it both captures clearly the essence of her concern and provides a good starting point for group discussion. See Chapter 5.)
- Should all participants have their own copies of the work samples, or can they share the originals?
- Should the students' names be removed or covered up? (Groups have different norms about identifying students.)

Feedback from the facilitator at any stage in the preparation process (selecting work, framing questions, choosing a protocol, or drafting a presentation) can be extremely helpful. The facilitator may try to anticipate the group's response to the presentation: "From the group's point of view, I feel like it would be helpful to . . . " However, whether speaking for herself or for the group, the facilitator should try to stay clear of opinions and judgments and strive for questions that help the presenter clarify her own idea of what will push her learning and the group's.

AFTER THE MEETING

Although the protocol itself lasts a relatively short time, the learning opportunities that it generates may continue to emerge long after the protocol is over. While it is up to the presenter and group members to apply to their own work what they have learned in the discussion, facilitators can do some things to support this ongoing learning and encourage changes in practice for participants.

Even before the meeting ends, the facilitator can engage the group in reflection. This can be as simple as taking time at the end of the meeting for ideas or questions about how the discussion will affect the classroom. She might pose questions such as, "What will you continue to think about or wrestle with?" or, "As a participant, what did you hear that got you thinking about your own classroom?" Sometimes these questions are already built into the protocol (in the reflection or debriefing stage), or they might become part of a discussion after the protocol or several protocols.

Other ways of supporting continued reflection and learning take place immediately after the meeting or, ideally, between meetings. These include

- *Checking in with the presenter.* This is often informal, beginning with a question like, "What did you hear?" (rather than, "What are you going to do now?"). Even if this kind of check is built into the protocol, the facilitator might want to find a time after the meeting to touch base with the presenter once they have both had more time to digest the group's conversation.

- *Thinking ahead to the next meeting.* Participants can begin to give shape to their initial ideas about changes in practice by visualizing what kinds of student or teacher work (or other materials) they might bring to a future meeting to make those changes visible for the group. While it may be too early for group members to make definite selection decisions, the facilitator might spur their thinking by asking, "What kinds of work or materials might you bring to the next meeting that would help us reflect on and discuss something you have tried that relates to our discussion today?"

- *Sharing documentation.* Facilitators may document meetings in a variety of ways and at different levels. In some groups, a recorder may take charge of documentation. However a meeting is documented, it can be helpful to the presenter and other participants to receive a brief summary of the meeting that captures the highlights: the presenter(s), the question(s) or issue(s) focused on, the materials presented, the protocol(s) used, and some of the identifiable outcomes, for example, some of the possibilities discussed for changes in practice and decisions made about future presenters, questions, or kinds of work to present.

*   *   *

Facilitators can never foresee everything that will happen in the actual protocol. However, thinking of preparation for a protocol as a critical part of the presenter's and the group's learning process—a process that also encompasses the protocol itself and reflections after it—can extend the possibilities for deeper individual and group learning. Seeing the protocol as part of a larger trajectory of learning also can support the facilitator's own learning about facilitation and how to do it more effectively, with greater satisfaction.

Chapter 7

How Do Facilitators Choose, Adapt, and Create Protocols?

In the previous chapter, we introduced the idea that deciding which protocol to use is one crucial consideration in planning for a protocol-guided discussion of student and/or teacher work. Different kinds of protocols serve different purposes and support exploration of different questions that presenters frame. With several dozen protocols currently in widespread use around the country (at last count!), knowing which to use is not always easy. In this chapter, we consider how facilitators work with presenters and groups to choose a protocol that will best serve both the presenter's and the group's questions and goals.

Even after the protocol has been chosen and the group has launched into it, situations arise that call for making adjustments in midconversation. Deciding when and how to make such adjustments is an important part of the facilitator's work that we discuss later in this chapter. Finally, since even the current collection of well-established protocols won't satisfy every issue or need a group identifies, we also share some thoughts about the process of developing or adapting a protocol to suit specific contexts and needs.

CHOOSING AN APPROPRIATE PROTOCOL

Just as different tools in the toolbox are used for different tasks, so different protocols allow groups to accomplish different goals. Figure 7.1 lists three popular—and very different—protocols and highlights some of the differences evident in their purposes and structures. Of course, there are many other protocols that groups might consider, but these three provide a good representation of the range of purposes and structures of protocols. Chapter 1 includes all three protocols as well as a tool (Figure 1.1) for identifying the purposes and likely outcomes of a protocol based on its features (whether the protocol calls for a focusing question, whether context for the work is shared before or after the group's conversation about the work, and so on).

The chart in Figure 7.1 can serve as a starting point for exploring these protocols and their most effective uses. It also can help in pre-conference conversations between the presenter and facilitator (and, sometimes, the entire group) about which protocol will best address the presenter's framing question and selected work. There is no formula for matching purpose to protocol. The process can be thought of as a kind of conversational triangulation: trying to find the protocol that is most likely to connect the presenter's framing question or interest, the work she has selected to present, and the group's purposes.

It may be helpful to visualize such a conversation: The presenter and the facilitator sit together at a table with samples of student work and teacher-created documents from an assignment or a project laid out in front of them—more samples than ultimately may be presented. They have the protocol continua from Figure 1.1 and the overview chart from Figure 7.1 at hand. They also have more detailed descriptions of protocols from websites like those maintained by the Looking at Student Work Collaborative (www.lasw.org) and the National School Reform Faculty's New York Center (www.nsrfnewyork.org) as well as print resources like *The Power of Protocols* (McDonald et al., 2003) and *The Evidence Process* (Evidence Project Staff, 2001). With a pad of paper handy to capture possible focusing questions, the two play out some scenarios: "If we were to use the Collaborative Assessment Conference, which piece of work might you choose? Why?" or, "Given your [the presenter's] interest in students developing research questions, which of the protocols seems most appropriate? Why?"

Sometimes, as part of the preconference conversations, facilitators share helpful rules of thumb. For example, if the presenting teacher's interest seems to gravitate to the assignment or assessment tool, a Tuning Protocol or similar context-first protocol may be called for. If the presenter's interest seems to be sparked by a particular student's work, a more descriptive protocol, like the Collaborative Assessment Conference, may be more appropriate. Such guidelines are helpful but should not cut short the triangulation conversation, since these con-

Figure 7.1. Overview of the Three Protocols

Purpose	Kinds of Work Presented	Brief Summary of Steps	Facilitator Role
Collaborative Assessment Conference *			
To give the presenter a fresh perspective on a student's work, particularly when the presenter is genuinely wondering about—or is baffled by—the work and/or the student. To promote understanding about that student as a learner and creator within a specific discipline or domain and to spark thinking about teaching and learning issues that apply to other students, classrooms, and disciplines.	Student work that was created in response to a relatively open-ended assignment. Usually a single piece of work from an individual student; sometimes several pieces of work from the same student.	• Presenter provides no context initially. • Colleagues describe the work. • Colleagues raise a variety of questions about the work. • Colleagues speculate about the student's intentions in creating the work. • Presenter shares context and reflects on the conversation she has heard. • Colleagues and presenter discuss implications for their own practice. • Everyone debriefs the process.	*Before the protocol*: Helps the presenter understand she will have no input into the protocol until late in the process; no contextual information is given to the group before they begin their discussion. *During the protocol*: Helps participants to understand difference between description, interpretation, and evaluation to enable them to describe the work without evaluating or judging it. Helps participants steer away from advice giving and toward reflection on their own teaching and learning.
Consultancy **			
To help the presenter think more expansively about a professional dilemma or problem she is facing through offering other points of view and other possibilities.	Usually a written description of the dilemma, though sometimes a verbal one. Educator work or students' work may be presented to provide context for the dilemma, but the focus is on the dilemma (as opposed to the work).	• Presenter gives overview of the dilemma. • Presenter provides a focusing question. • Colleagues ask clarifying and probing questions. • Colleagues provide feedback designed to give the presenter new perspectives/ideas. • Presenter responds. • Everyone debriefs the process.	*Before the protocol:* Works with the presenter to shape the dilemma and discuss how it will be shared with the group. It is critical that the presenter thinks a solution to dilemma is possible but doesn't know what it is; and that the presenter is willing to change her own practice to resolve the dilemma. *During the protocol*: Helps participants appreciate the distinction between "probing questions" and those that ask for more information, offer recommendations, or imply solutions.

(continued)

Figure 7.1. *(continued)*

Purpose	Kinds of Work Presented	Brief Summary of Steps	Facilitator Role
Tuning Protocol ***			
To help the presenter "fine-tune" an assignment, task, project design, or assessment tool, often in relation to an explicit standard.	Usually the presenter's assignment and/or assessment tool and multiple samples (normally 3-5) of student work that responded to the assignment or were assessed with the assessment tool. Student work samples usually demonstrate different levels of accomplishment. Can also be used for looking at samples of teacher work (such as lesson plans, project designs, and so on).	• Presenter provides initial explanation of the context, student learning goals, assignment, and assessment format. • Presenter identifies a framing question. • Colleagues ask clarifying questions. • Colleagues examine work. • Colleagues provide "warm" and "cool" feedback while presenter listens. • Presenter reflects on feedback. • Everyone debriefs the process.	*Before the protocol*: Helps the presenter develop a focusing question that is important to the presenter herself and will prompt rich feedback, both warm and cool. *During the protocol*: Helps participants recognize the value of (and forms for) warm and cool feedback.

Note: Adapted from charts created by Gene Thompson-Grove, National School Reform Faculty, February 2002

* Developed by Steve Seidel and colleagues at Harvard Project Zero, 1988.

** Originally developed as part of the Coalition of Essential Schools' National Re:Learning Program; further adapted and revised by Gene Thompson-Grove and colleagues in the National School Reform Faculty (NSRF).

*** Developed by Joseph McDonald at the Coalition of Essential Schools, 1991. Revised by David Allen

versations can themselves be opportunities for learning about student and teacher work, as well as about protocols.

Of course, this kind of conversation also might happen in groups, especially more experienced ones, at the beginning of a meeting to which the presenter has brought samples of work and a good idea about why she would like to discuss them with the group. Appendix B offers a "protocol-matching activity" that may be useful for groups to use early on in their work together to explore the dimensions of choosing a protocol.

Trial and error also play a role: While the selected protocol may not turn out to be the best one for the presenter's particular question or selected work, reflecting on how it did and did not match the presenter's and group's goals also can add to the group's knowledge of protocols and their uses.

MAKING ADJUSTMENTS, ADAPTING PROTOCOLS, AND CREATING NEW PROTOCOLS

Are protocol structures sacred cows or fair game? Different facilitators have different philosophies about how gingerly to treat a protocol. Some feel that the steps of a protocol need to be followed precisely at all times in order to achieve the maximum benefit. In their view, it is the discipline of the protocol that enables powerful and wide-ranging ideas to emerge. Other facilitators—we among them—see the value, at times, of thoughtfully modifying a protocol in progress in order to respond to the emerging needs of a particular group or situation. These facilitators are also more likely to endorse adapting (or "tinkering with") familiar protocols for particular professional contexts, purposes, kinds of work to be presented, and so on. And, of course, some occasions and purposes may call for the development of an entirely new protocol.

Modifying, adapting, or creating a protocol requires thoughtfulness and attention to detail. Protocols perform complex functions in shaping and guiding a group's experience. A protocol assists the group in reaching some purposes, while ruling out others. Its features determine the ways in which group members will interact and, through the various qualities of that interaction, create a set of balances that contribute to the tone and substance of the conversation. As described in Chapter 1, the protocol often serves as a kind of co-facilitator in supporting the group's work. For all these reasons, we tend to be cautious in making changes to existing protocols and in developing new ones. Nevertheless, when undertaken with a healthy respect for the complexities entailed, modifying, adapting, and creating protocols can be satisfying and productive.

In the following sections, we look in more detail at what is involved, from a facilitator's point of view, in making adjustments in the midst of a protocol and in adapting a protocol or developing an entirely new one.

Making Adjustments in Mid-Protocol

In reading a group as it goes through a protocol, facilitators sometimes feel they need to make changes to a protocol on the spot. Facilitators may find themselves in the midst of a protocol that is not meeting the needs of the presenting teacher or the group. In this case, it may make sense to make adjustments to the protocol in order to address the emerging needs.

Before making structural changes in the protocol, the facilitator should try to determine whether the problem stems from a gap in understanding of the purpose of the protocol or of a particular step of the protocol. For issues of clarification, a range of moves will help the group get clearer about the purpose without altering the protocol structure (see Chapter 4).

Some instances, however, call for a more structural response. Perhaps the most common of these situations has to do with time. When a facilitator recognizes that a group would benefit from more time in a particular step (e.g., looking at student work samples), she may need to add time to this step and look for steps down the line that might be "shaved" by a minute or two to compensate. Conversely, facilitators develop skills in "banking" time: If a group completes an early step ahead of time, the facilitator may tack on a few minutes to a later step that would benefit from more time.

Another situation that can be treated structurally is the discovery, by the facilitator or the group, that the protocol doesn't provide for certain information at the point where it would be most helpful. For example, a facilitator may discover in a Tuning Protocol that participants do not have enough clarity about the samples of student work to offer the kinds of feedback the presenting teacher has requested. In this case, the facilitator might add another round of clarifying questions or the provision of additional context by the presenting teacher. It is usually helpful to suggest parameters for the inserted step, for example, "Let's take just three or four new clarifying questions at this point."

Another modification involves altering the order of steps of a protocol. It may become clear in beginning a Tuning Protocol, for example, that a review of the student work samples before hearing the context for the work might be beneficial. In this case, the facilitator might ask the presenter if the new order would be acceptable to her and explicitly mark for the group that the standard protocol is being adjusted.

We suggest a few points a facilitator might keep in mind if she decides to improvise in the midst of a protocol:

- *Recognize the integrity of the protocol you are modifying.* Protocols are structured to support particular kinds of inter-action to achieve particular purposes; modifications may affect those interactions in ways that diminish the protocol's capacity to achieve its objectives. For example, letting the pre-senting teacher in a Collaborative Assessment Conference give just a bit of context about the student at the beginning of the protocol will prevent participants from approaching the work with fresh eyes; allowing the presenting teacher in a Tuning Protocol to enter into dialogue with a participant during the "warm" and "cool" feedback step will undermine the (rare) opportunity for a teacher to listen, without reacting, to others discuss a question close to her heart.
- *Be conscious of what you're doing.* Simply "going with the flow" in a passive way does not count as facilitation in most proto-cols! Rather than allowing the conversation to drift away from the protocol, be conscious of when that "drift" is creeping in and make a decision about whether to allow the movement away from the protocol or to bring it back.
- *Mark the change for the group.* Changing a protocol in mid-stream means changing the ground rules by which the group has agreed to work (at least for that particular protocol). It is important to acknowledge the change explicitly—and per-haps even invite the group's thoughts about whether the change is the right move to make.
- *Discuss the adjustment in concrete terms in the debriefing peri-od.* If you do make a change in how the protocol normally is structured (or facilitated), be sure to invite the group's reflec-tions on those changes in the debrief step: "How did the change work for the group?" "What were the strengths and drawbacks of the change?" "Do you think it is worth trying the protocol this way again in the future?" An adjustment made once to respond to a particular situation may lead to a more formal adaptation of an established protocol for future uses.

Nearly every protocol we know has benefited from thoughtful experimentation and adaptation. Some of this happens "in the moment," while the protocol is underway. As we discuss in the next section, other adaptations and experiments are more deliberate.

Adapting a Protocol or Creating a New Protocol

A facilitator of a group that is using protocols to learn from student and teacher work may find, upon reflection, that she and/or the group members experience some dissatisfaction with a protocol the group has tried. In response, the facilitator (or others) might be inclined to make significant changes to the protocol or create a new one. Adapting a protocol might involve taking one of the modifications discussed above and using it with a group more intentionally, that is, in a planned way rather than as a response-in-the-moment. Creating a new protocol requires a more extensive development process that proceeds from identifying the purpose to designing and explicating the steps of the new protocol.

While either of these options could be productive, our experience suggests that a facilitator might want to try the following things first:

- *Talk to the group.* Whether the group, or you, or all of you together are sensing a problem with the protocol being used, a candid conversation is an important step toward identifying and understanding the issues. Almost every protocol has a built-in "debriefing" step at the end of it. Be sure to leave enough time for this step!
- *Give the protocol some time.* Protocols, by their nature, place restrictions on the natural flow of conversation. This is not always comfortable for participants, and this discomfort might be at the root of the group's dissatisfaction. If this is a possibility, getting familiar with a protocol by doing it a few times might be the best strategy. Furthermore, protocols, like any complex tool, take a bit of practice in order to be used effectively. So it might take a few tries before you and your group figure out just what your chosen protocol can really help you achieve and what it can't. Sometimes tinkering with small things in how the group uses the protocol (e.g., acting

on ideas that have come up in debriefing earlier uses) can make a big difference in the group's satisfaction.

- *Try another "established" protocol.* If lack of experience with protocols in general, or with the particular protocol you've chosen, isn't the problem, it might be that you have chosen a protocol that doesn't fit well with your group's needs or purposes. It might be worth revisiting (and perhaps revising) goals with the group, and then experimenting with some other protocols. (See Figure 7.1 and references cited in this chapter for more information on protocols and their uses.)
- *Talk to an experienced facilitator.* A conversation with someone who has used the protocol frequently can help you pinpoint some possible areas of difficulty and come up with some strategies for dealing with them.

When a facilitator and/or group decides to adapt an existing protocol or create a brand-new one, they need to address two kinds of issues: (1) conceptual issues having to do with how the new protocol is constructed, and (2) record-keeping and reference issues having to do with how the protocol is shared with others.

Conceptual Issues

Good protocols can take a long time to develop. Most of the protocols in popular use now have been through many rounds of experimentation and revision. As discussed in Chapter 1, the design of effective protocols creates particular balances among competing needs, interests, and inclinations. Because of these delicate balances, seemingly small changes in a protocol's steps can create big changes in the kind of conversations people have and, therefore, in the kinds of things they can accomplish with the protocol. When adapting or creating a protocol, here are some questions to think about:

- *What is your purpose?* What do you and your group want to accomplish through the protocol? Why is it important to the participants to talk together about their work in their classrooms? Are you seeking to open up and explore issues broadly? Or are you hoping to solve specific problems? Do you want the students' work or the teacher's work (or some mixture of

the two) to be the focus of the conversation? The other questions on this list should be considered in light of your
responses to this question about purposes.

- *How will your protocol balance opportunities for people both to
  express their own perspectives and to consider the perspectives of
  others?* Typically, this is done through a careful orchestration
  of who can talk and when. Does the presenter or the group
  start the conversation? Does the presenter or the group have
  the "last word" (before the debriefing step, in which everyone
  participates)? Is there a time when the presenter and group
  should talk together, or should one always be listening while
  the other is speaking?
- *When (if at all) will context for the work be shared?* Knowing
  or not knowing the context for the student work presented
  (e.g., the assignment, the scoring criteria, information about
  the student, and so on) has a profound effect on how participants see and respond to the work. Will this sort of context be
  provided at the beginning of the conversation? In the middle?
  Only at the end? Never?
- *How will your protocol balance free conversation and structured
  responses?* Protocols typically ask people to respond in specific ways to the work that is on the table. At what points will
  your protocol invite very focused conversation (e.g., certain
  kinds of questions or feedback)? At what points will it invite
  more open-ended, less focused conversation?
- *How will steps be organized and timed?* Once larger questions
  of purposes and roles are determined, consider other important issues such as: What sequence of steps makes the most
  sense? How much time (approximately) should be devoted to
  each step?

Even though these questions ask how to balance various needs, all
these needs do not have to be given equal time in every protocol. For
example, depending on your purposes, you might construct a protocol
that allows for lots of group talk and very little presenter talk, or vice
versa. The point here is not to argue that all needs have to be met equally in every protocol, but rather to encourage deliberate choices about
which needs will be given prominence and how.

Record-Keeping and Reference Issues

As discussed, protocol developers (individuals and organizations) have different perspectives on how their protocols are used by others. While some are happy to see their work freely used and adapted, others are particularly concerned that the protocols they create are used according to the guidelines they established. However, most of us agree that when using or adapting a protocol, careful attribution of the source is appropriate and helpful.

If a facilitator decides to adapt a protocol or create a new one, we recommend using the following guidelines when committing the adapted or new protocol to paper or website (even in draft form):

- *Give the protocol a name.* Things can get confusing when two, three, or more very different sets of steps are all named "The Tuning Protocol." When you make a significant adaptation or create a new protocol, give it a name that will distinguish it from other protocols. (For instance, the "California Protocol" is an adaptation of the "Tuning Protocol.")
- *Identify the protocol you are adapting or deriving your protocol from.* For example, the Modified Collaborative Assessment Conference includes in its description the attribution: "A variation of the Collaborative Assessment Conference developed by Steve Seidel at Harvard Project Zero."
- *Include your own name and/or your group's name on the new or adapted protocol, and date it.* You never know where your protocol might end up once you've put it in writing or on the web. It can be helpful to let people know where it came from so that they can get in touch with you if they have questions about how to use it (or to share some insights that emerged from using it). Providing a date helps people sort out different versions of the same or similar protocols.
- *Include with the protocol a statement of its purpose or the goals it is intended to achieve.* Describing in brief the purpose of the protocol is an important aid to others who are trying to decide which protocol to use in addressing their group's needs and goals. (See Figure 7.1 for examples of brief statements of purpose for protocols.)

*   *   *

One of the lessons that has emerged most strongly for us in facilitating and studying protocols for looking at student and teacher work is that it is all too easy to lose track of the purpose for using protocols, even as we get caught up in doing them. Whether a facilitator is choosing a protocol to use, modifying one in midstream, or developing a new one, the question of purpose should be kept on the table for all participants to appreciate.

Chapter 8

What Are the Challenges of Facilitating Protocols?

While protocols contribute to positive and productive meetings with opportunities for individual and group learning, they can be challenging to facilitate. Overcoming these challenges should be one of the most interesting aspects of the facilitator's responsibilities—and one that contributes powerfully to her learning about facilitation and about herself as a facilitator.

In this chapter, we identify some of those challenges. For any significant challenge that emerges in a protocol, no single solution exists. Each challenge is influenced by many contextual variables, including who is in the group, what its goals are, who is presenting, which protocol is being used, and so on. Addressing the challenge requires applying the dispositions discussed in Chapter 3 (reading the situation and the group; determining what kind of response, if any, is called for; and reflecting on how the challenge was met and what can be learned for future conversations) as well as the moves considered in Chapter 4.

In this chapter we address the following common challenges that facilitators encounter in protocols:

- Time is running out.
- The group is too big.
- Participants have a hard time sticking with the protocol.
- Participants rush to evaluate or judge the work being presented.
- Participants seem reluctant to offer challenging feedback.
- The presenting teacher's presentation wanders or expands.
- The presenting teacher uses her response time for something other than response.

- Participants turn to other participants, or to the facilitator, as an expert on the content.
- The facilitator is uncertain whether to participate in the content of the conversation or stick to facilitating the process.
- The facilitator feels a bit hesitant or unsure of her skills.
- One or more participants resist participating in the protocol.

Of course, an exhaustive list would be impossible: The challenges each group faces vary according to their contexts, participants, and goals. Rather, we hope to provide a flavor for the kinds of issues that can crop up. For each challenge, we suggest some possible reasons for its emergence and some forms it may take in the conversation. We also consider a range of responses facilitators may want to think about in addressing each challenge, leaving decisions about specific moves to the reader.

Each section below begins with a very brief sketch of a typical scenario in which a particular challenge is likely to surface. Appendix B offers more detailed scenarios as part of an activity that asks facilitators to "read" potentially tricky situations and respond to them with moves that support a productive, positive conversation for the whole group.

TIME IS RUNNING OUT

During a step of the protocol that calls for discussion among the participants, you (the facilitator) become deeply absorbed in the conversation. You glance at your watch and realize that you have less than 15 minutes left for the group to cover the last four steps of the protocol . . .

Protocols help structure a full, purposeful conversation within a limited period of time. For all kinds of reasons, the conversation may not fit neatly into the time allotted. For example, the group's meeting may start late because of a fire drill. Or the work samples may be so long (or numerous) that participants need extra time to read them. Or, after a complex or confusing presentation by a presenter, the group may need extra time for clarification questions in order to have a productive discussion. Or the facilitator may simply get caught up in the conversation and lose track of time. For all these reasons (and many others), facilitators nearly always have to make decisions about staying with a particular step in the protocol or moving on—even when the protocol being used has explicitly timed steps.

Rather than cut off conversation in the earlier steps of the protocol, facilitators sometimes make the decision to let those steps run longer and then compensate by "borrowing" time from later steps. However, this move is not always advisable. While it can be difficult to interrupt a conversation that is really cooking, moving ahead (before that part of the conversation is exhausted) can create momentum and carry energy into subsequent steps. This involves a little faith on the facilitator's part that the conversation will benefit from being jogged ahead. Sometimes the facilitator can help the group (and herself) move forward by acknowledging to the group the trade-off involved in moving on. Ultimately, facilitators develop ways to "work" the protocol and the clock in order to support conversations that are full yet do not feel rushed—but of course this takes time!

THE GROUP IS TOO BIG

> Your school is just beginning to explore protocols as a way to support teachers' professional development. As someone who is helping to organize this work, you hold an initial meeting for anyone who is interested to come and experience a protocol that you will facilitate. As the room fills up to overflowing, you are both pleasantly surprised and increasingly worried: How will you manage such a large group of beginners?

Protocols benefit from a diversity of perspectives. Larger groups certainly bring that diversity but also may bring challenges, for example, in allowing everybody to be heard or moving through all the steps in a timely manner or in the facilitator's ability to read individual participants' engagement in and comprehension of the process.

It may be obvious that a group's size is straining the capacity of the process if the participants don't fit around the table or overfill the space you have in which to meet. However, the effects of size may become apparent in other, subtler ways, for example, when time constraints make it difficult for everybody who wants to participate to do so within a certain part of the conversation, or when some participants seem to be "mentally dropping out" while others are still fully engaged (of course, this is not always caused by group size alone).

While it is certainly preferable to work with an optimally sized group (for us, 6 to 12 people), situations do arise when larger groups meet. These can be productive conversations but may call for making some adjustments. Facilitators often respond to such situations by looking for ways to encourage participation by everybody in the group. Sometimes this might mean creating space, through an explicit invitation, for those who haven't spoken yet (or spoken much): "Let's leave some time now for anyone who hasn't already done so to say something if they'd like to."

Facilitators also may build into particular steps of the protocol the opportunity for participants to talk first to one another in small groups or pairs for a few minutes. (This allows participants who are less comfortable speaking in larger groups to be heard.) Or facilitators simply might acknowledge the size of the group as a challenge and ask for the group's help in having a conversation that includes everybody, stays focused, and moves ahead.

PARTICIPANTS HAVE A HARD TIME STICKING WITH THE PROTOCOL

The protocol you are facilitating calls first for a presentation from the presenting teacher and then a round of clarifying questions. But when the time for clarifying questions arrives, several group members dive in with substantive feedback or probing questions. When you try to steer them toward clarifying questions, "asking for more nuts-and-bolts kinds of information," some participants are able to adjust their participation, but a few do not seem to understand what you are asking for. You encounter similar difficulties with each successive step of the protocol . . .

Protocols provide guidance about how group members should participate at different points in the conversation. Participants' lack of understanding can lead to a mismatch between their comments and what is called for by the protocol, for example, asking probing questions during a period that calls for clarifying questions, or critiquing rather than describing a piece of student work. Participants may be baffled by the unusual constraints protocols put on conversation and become confused about what kind of participation is appropriate. An out-of-place comment also might reflect the participant's conviction that her comments may be more helpful (or necessary) at a particular point than what the protocol actually calls for. (Very rarely does such behavior signal a willful resistance to the protocol, the group's purpose, or the facilitation; see below for a discussion of when it might.) Furthermore, facilitators themselves sometimes struggle to determine whether a particular comment or question is what the protocol asks for in a given step (e.g., in determining whether a comment is descriptive or interpretive, or a question is clarifying or probing).

When facilitators read gaps in understanding in one or more participants, they might respond in ways that seek to lower anxiety and increase understanding. They might, for example, review the general purposes and process of the protocol, clarify specific aspects of the protocol structure, or model what is called for in a part of the protocol that is confusing or unclear. When a facilitator herself is unsure about whether a particular comment belongs in a step, she simply might check briefly with the participants about their thoughts. Or she might choose to "think out loud" to reveal her own process for determining whether a comment is in keeping with the protocol's guidelines.

Of course, the goal of a protocol isn't to have participants reading off a script or biting their tongues rather than risk a comment or question that isn't precisely what the protocol calls for. The point is to have a productive discussion, not a perfectly executed protocol. While a facilitator should do what she can to help each participant to understand, she also must consider the group's interest. Sometimes a facilitator may decide to "live with" a participant who isn't totally up to speed in order to keep the conversation moving. There are usually opportunities after a meeting to talk to an individual participant who still may be struggling with the purposes or process for the conversation. Fortunately, all protocols have a certain amount of give built in, and a small number of off-topic comments are unlikely to derail the whole process.

PARTICIPANTS RUSH TO EVALUATE OR JUDGE THE WORK BEING PRESENTED

> You are facilitating a protocol that calls for the group members to make purely descriptive comments about the work. Yet a number of people can't seem to resist offering evaluations of the quality of the work. Each time, you steer them back toward description by saying over and over (or so it seems to you), "What do you see in the work that makes you say that?" You can tell that one or two of them are getting a bit irritated . . .

This challenge is a more specific version of the previous one, but it turns up often enough to merit particular attention: Even when participants understand the purposes for protocols and see their value, some protocols invite certain kinds of participation that group members find especially challenging. In particular, several protocols (such as the Collaborative Assessment Conference and the Descriptive Review processes) require participants to withhold judgment or evaluation, focusing instead on observing and describing the work in specific and factual terms. This kind of participation is often difficult: Judgment and evaluation are so much a part of what educators do on a daily basis with their students' work that it may be hard to imagine an extended conversation without them. However, that is exactly what many protocols ask participants to do in order to open up different kinds of conversations and opportunities for learning.

When a judgmental or an evaluative comment or question (e.g., "Why didn't you do it this way?) is offered out of place, facilitators' responses vary. A facilitator might ask for the evidence that prompted the comment or question ("What do you see in the work that leads you to say that?"). Some make a similar point by straightforwardly stating their own (momentary) "cluelessness": "I guess I'm just not seeing where that idea is coming from. Can you point out a specific example in the work?" Facilitators also might pause the protocol for a moment to discuss with the group the challenges of withholding judgment; or they might, for a variety of reasons, choose not to say anything.

Facilitators sometimes can preempt or reduce such problems by addressing the issue before the protocol begins. Simply discussing

ahead of time the distinctions among observation, description, interpretation, and evaluation can help. A facilitator also can let people
know at the start of the protocol or the relevant step that judgments are
likely to creep into the conversation and alert them to the kinds of
things she'll say to steer them back toward observation. Other facilitators have developed activities for having participants practice offering
different kinds of comments about the same object (e.g., a poster in the
room) as a way to help them distinguish among description, interpretation, and evaluation.

PARTICIPANTS SEEM RELUCTANT TO
OFFER CHALLENGING FEEDBACK

The group has been in the "warm and cool" feedback step of the
Tuning Protocol for 6 or 7 minutes when you notice that people
seem to be choosing their words very carefully—and that most of
what they're saying doesn't seem especially substantive or probing. You begin to think that in their efforts to "be nice," they're taking the power out of this part of the conversation . . .

This challenge is, in some ways, the opposite of the "rushing to evaluation" problem. In some groups or in some circumstances, participants
might hesitate to raise questions or offer feedback, including comments
on samples of student work, that might appear to be critical of the presenting teacher. Facilitators may hesitate to encourage more probing or
challenging questions and feedback because it might risk moving people out of their "comfort zone."

While this hesitation may derive from any number of sources, it
reflects a truism of the teaching profession: Rarely are teachers called
upon to critique one another. Consequently, teachers in general are not
used to either giving or receiving critique. Conversations about practice
tend to be polite and abstract, or marked by storytelling rather than
analysis. This is one of the reasons protocols have proved so helpful to
groups of teachers: They are a tool for getting below the surface of civil
but not particularly thought-provoking conversations.

Generally, as a group uses protocols over time to look at student and
teacher work, a level of trust develops that allows participants to
become more comfortable both with presenting their work and their

students' work and with sharing their perspectives on the work of other participants. In the early going, however, it is natural for a presenter to share work that, in her estimation, went particularly well, and for participants to be shy about offering feedback. It is also natural for participants to hold back "edgier" feedback or questions.

To help groups (and individual participants) become more comfortable with—and gain practice in—sharing perspectives that provide useful critique, the facilitator may use a number of strategies before the protocol begins. For example, in discussing group norms, it may be useful to talk explicitly about the value of critique (and ways it may be offered positively). Courtney Cazden (2001) captures the distinction between criticism and critique this way:

- Criticism is about finished work; critique is about work still in progress.
- Criticism is often given by persons who do it as their primary job (such as film critics for a newspaper); critique is a temporary role offered by one artist to another.
- Criticism is one-way, from the critic to creator and potential audience; critique is a two-way, reciprocal relationship. (p. 116)

No matter how thoroughly a group discusses norms, the facilitator still may discover in the midst of the protocol that the group is "walking on eggshells" with the presenter. In such a case, she can refer to the protocol as a co-facilitator, pointing out that it calls for a certain kind of question or feedback at this point, and relieving participants of the appearance of aggressive criticism. ("Look, this is what the protocol asks for at this point; it may feel a bit awkward, but let's give it a try.") The facilitator also might decide to provide a bit of judicious modeling or to reference the criticism–critique distinction mentioned above.

The facilitator also may use carefully framed questions to help participants offer feedback that is neither so bland that it provokes no new thinking nor so aggressive that it stuns the presenter. Some of the most helpful questions or prompts from the facilitator, in such cases, are those that call for description, rather than interpretation; these tend to support a positive tone, allow participants to offer observations without fear of appearing critical, and contribute to a deeper understanding of the work.

In meeting with the presenter before the protocol, facilitators often try to get a sense of the kind of feedback and critique a presenter is asking for and prepared to take in. The facilitator then can use questions and, perhaps, modeling during the protocol to find a balance between affirming comments and more probing or provocative feedback.

THE PRESENTING TEACHER'S PRESENTATION WANDERS OR EXPANDS

In the protocol you are facilitating, the first step is the presentation from the teacher who has brought work. She begins by describing the assignment but quickly seems to wander into a kind of stream-of-consciousness description of various students' backgrounds: "This is one of the most interesting classes I've ever had. I had students from, I think, seven different countries. This one little girl . . ."

Presenting in a protocol usually involves making one's work and/or one's students' work highly visible to a group of colleagues. With this visibility comes a degree of vulnerability that, for many teachers, is unfamiliar and therefore somewhat uncomfortable. The presenting teacher's very understandable need to make sure that her work is understood, and her desire to hear that that work is valued by colleagues, sometimes can make it difficult for her to stick with the protocol and participate in ways that will further the work of the group.

In a protocol that designates an initial presentation time, the presenting teacher might be inclined to slip into show-and-tell mode, with emphasis on how well the work went, rather than on inviting questions and other perspectives on the work. Sometimes, presenting teachers try to squeeze in every last bit of information about the work, the students, the class, and so on, rather than being focused and selective.

This is the kind of challenge that is best anticipated and addressed in the preconference (see Chapter 6). The facilitator can help the presenter prepare both mentally and practically for the challenge of making her work visible to colleagues in a way that invites the group to participate in a substantive discussion of the work and related issues of teaching and learning. However, when a lack of focus becomes evident during the presentation itself, the facilitator might need to gently remind the presenter to return to the information most relevant for the group, if only because time requires it.

THE PRESENTING TEACHER USES HER RESPONSE TIME FOR SOMETHING OTHER THAN RESPONSE

When the time comes for the presenting teacher to reflect on what she has heard in the group conversation, she begins by correcting misperceptions that emerged in the conversation and providing as much information about the context as she can. She goes on to explain that she has already tried most of the ideas the group has mentioned and that she would never be able to do the ones she hasn't already tried ("If you knew what my school is like . . . "). As the minutes tick by, you realize that she is focused on defending her work, rather than on drawing new perspectives or ideas from the conversation . . .

While not all protocols require that presenting teachers share the context for the work at the beginning of the conversation, virtually all protocols provide for a step, at or near the end of the protocol, in which the presenting teacher reflects out loud on what she heard in the conversation. This step can pose a serious challenge to the presenting teacher. It requires that she resist the very natural tendencies to become defensive about the work and/or to try to respond to every question raised by the group (for fear that they will leave not understanding completely everything that she and her students did in the task or project being discussed). The response time in most protocols is much more productive when the presenter uses it to reflect on new perspectives she has gained and identify a few ideas about which she would like to ponder further.

Many facilitators find it helpful to acknowledge in both the preconference and the protocol itself that the presenting teacher's role in this particular step is a tough one. The presenting teacher may feel reassured when the facilitator underscores (perhaps just before the step in which the presenter responds) that it is not the presenter's responsibility to clear up all the misconceptions that inevitably will have emerged in the group's conversation. Nor does the presenter need to answer all the questions the group has raised. Rather, she need only think aloud about what she heard, perhaps identifying a new perspective the conversation might have sparked for her or a new idea about something she might want to try in her classroom.

Of course, in the pressure of the moment, even the best-prepared presenters may find themselves slipping into less productive ways of responding. The situation may require the facilitator to gently interrupt and tactfully remind the presenter of her own focusing question or the purposes of this particular part of the protocol.

PARTICIPANTS TURN TO OTHER PARTICIPANTS, OR TO THE FACILITATOR, AS AN EXPERT ON THE CONTENT

> You are facilitating a protocol in which the group is examining samples of student writing. During the discussion period, a participant in the group, known in the school as a writing specialist, begins to share a list of effective strategies from a program for which she is a trainer. The group listens attentively . . .

Sometimes a participant will emerge, through her comments, as an "expert" in the area under discussion. Alternatively, participants may turn to the facilitator with the expectation that she will be able to resolve complex issues or name the next strategies that the presenter should try in her classroom. While the facilitator or someone else in the group may indeed have particular expertise and useful suggestions or guidance for the presenter, allowing the group to focus exclusively on that expertise may foreclose the possibility that other perspectives and ideas will be introduced and explored. In addition, such a narrow focus on problem solving may limit the participants' ability to explore and deepen their understanding of the problems or questions either posed to the group by the presenter or inherent in the work itself.

Participants sometimes air expertise through storytelling ("I did a unit like this once . . . ") or even through questions that, nominally intended to solicit information or probe the presenter's thinking, are suggestions in disguise ("Have you tried . . . ?"). For the facilitator, responding to these situations can be tricky, and made even trickier if the presenter or group seems to be very receptive to the "expert" advice (as in the example above). A facilitator's range of responses might include: invoking the authority of the protocol in order to cut short the exclusive focus on one person's expertise ("The protocol suggests we get a range of feedback out on the table . . . "); redirecting the expert comments to a later, more appropriate point in the conversation; reminding the group of the purposes of the conversation; or making space for more people to be heard and more perspectives to be shared.

When the perceived expert is the facilitator, she can take steps to maintain her authority as a facilitator without becoming a magnet for the group's attention at the cost of more balanced and participatory conversation. For example, she might redirect back to the group questions that come to her. She also might monitor her own participation to make sure most of it is focused on facilitating.

THE FACILITATOR IS UNCERTAIN WHETHER TO PARTICIPATE IN THE CONTENT OF THE CONVERSATION OR STICK TO FACILITATING THE PROCESS

The feedback discussion is getting really interesting. So far you have focused all your comments and questions on facilitating the protocol, but you have a lot to say about the particular issue that has emerged in the discussion . . .

Different facilitators will respond to situations like this one differently. Some prefer to focus on the responsibilities of facilitation; others move comfortably between the role of facilitator and that of participant. Some find it helpful to be "transparent" and let the group know when they are "stepping out" of the facilitator's role to offer a question or comment. Early on in a group's work together, it can be especially helpful for the facilitator to be explicit about the role she is playing in the group.

For the facilitator, participating in the conversation has its risks: While she may be able to contribute to the group's understanding of the presenter's question and the work presented, participating in this way may make it more difficult for her to maintain a wider perspective on the conversation. This wider perspective—seeing both the forest *and* the trees—is essential. It allows the facilitator to read the whole group, as well as individuals' participation in the group. In addition, when a facilitator enters the conversation as a participant, "facilitator slippage" may occur: The facilitator may become so caught up in the conversation that she unintentionally relinquishes the role of facilitator and the protocol drifts or runs out of time.

As with all of these challenges, no one solution applies universally: Ultimately, each facilitator needs to determine for herself how she can best participate in the group.

THE FACILITATOR FEELS A BIT HESITANT OR UNSURE OF HER SKILLS

You are facilitating a protocol that's new for you and your group. A participant asks a question about the process: "Wouldn't it make more sense to get some more information about the students before we look at the work?" You begin to answer, then pause when you realize you don't have a good answer to offer . . .

Facilitation is not a performance, but, like teaching, it has an element of performance within it (Sarason, 1999). It doesn't require that the facilitator perform the steps of the protocol flawlessly, yet the group looks to her as the expert on the process. Situations do arise in which facilitators, especially more novice ones, feel a lack of confidence in their skills or doubt their judgment. They might, for example, find themselves thinking, "I don't know whether to interrupt the dialogue that's going on between the presenter and this particular participant—or how."

There is no substitute for time and practice in developing a greater command of the dispositions (described in Chapter 3) and specific moves (some of which are described in Chapter 4). Still, novice facilitators can facilitate very productive conversations if they trust themselves and the protocol.

Even experienced facilitators occasionally find that they feel lost in the middle of a protocol or that they question their ability to facilitate.

An awkward pause, a stray comment from a participant, a presenter who seems upset by what she is hearing—these and many other situations can spark a facilitator's self-doubt. In such moments, a facilitator might

- *Rely on the protocol.* Remind yourself and the group of the guidance offered in the protocol steps: "At this point the protocol calls for us to stick to clarifying questions, which are defined as . . . ." On the other hand, don't feel you have to defend the protocol against all charges (see Chapter 7 for a discussion of making adjustments in mid-protocol).
- *Ask for the group's input.* Sometimes protocol process questions can be addressed most helpfully by a brief group discussion of why it might make sense to follow the protocol or what exactly is meant by, for example, "probing question" or "cool feedback." While this strategy empowers the group, it is important not to lose sight of your own role in guiding the process—a facilitator that seems indecisive about every turn of events may lose the group's confidence in her facilitation skills and, perhaps, in the value of using a protocol at all.
- *Breathe! Don't let yourself feel rushed.* Facilitators should always reserve the right to take a moment to reflect on where the group is in the process, review the protocol guidelines, ask for input, and so on. When the facilitator pauses for this kind of reflection, she often announces to the group that she is doing so (which should relieve any discomfort the group might feel about her momentary silence).

In Chapter 9, we consider some of the ways novice facilitators—and more experienced ones—improve their work.

ONE OR MORE PARTICIPANTS DELIBERATELY RESIST PARTICIPATING IN THE PROTOCOL

You can't help but notice that one participant in the group has been doing a fair amount of eye-rolling and whispering to her neighbors during the early steps of the protocol. In the middle of the feedback period in the protocol, she finally cuts in with, "I just have to ask you [the presenter] one question, and then you can all go back to your protocol." . . .

With few exceptions, teachers value conversations with colleagues about teaching and learning, and share willingly in the responsibility for making such conversations constructive. Very occasionally, however, some participants—especially those who have never taken part in a protocol—resist the process.

Resistance usually can be handled without disrupting the protocol much, if at all, or calling attention to the participant who seems resistant. However, sometimes the level of resistance, or the particular form it takes, requires a more significant response from the facilitator. In this section, we consider three levels of resistance and ranges of responses facilitators may consider in addressing and, with a little luck, mitigating the resistance (if not always converting the resistor!).

Resistance may be motivated by any number of factors, from lack of clarity about the goals or process for the conversation to feeling coerced into participation. Discovering the source of the resistance can be helpful, although doing so in the midst of the conversation is not always possible—or advisable—since it can create a side show that overshadows the conversation the group set out to have. Of course, facilitators want to address individual concerns. However, they also must guard against allowing one person's concerns to edge out the identified and shared purposes of the group.

Passive Resistance

A participant may seem to withdraw from the conversation, but do so in a way that calls some attention to his/her withdrawal. While the facilitator's goal is to make sure all participants feel welcome to participate in the discussion, singling out an individual who seems to be withdrawing (e.g., by calling on him/her by name) can be risky. Facilitators may respond to this kind of resistance by inviting comments or questions from those who haven't had much to say yet (or in a while) or asking if anyone has any questions about the process of the protocol the group is using.

Of course, in spite of the facilitator's best efforts, the resisting participant might not take part in the conversation. In such a case, the facilitator may choose to check in privately with this participant after the meeting to see if she/he has any questions or concerns.

Testing

A participant may raise questions or make comments that, in effect, test the limits of the process. This testing may take the form of insisting on asking a question or making a comment during a period when such participation is not called for. For example, "I know we're supposed to be looking at the work but I just need to know . . . " or, "I feel I have to tell you that this work is probably copied from . . . " In response to this kind of testing, the facilitator might choose to ask the participant to hang onto the question or comment for later in the protocol; ask the group to "break protocol" for this one question or comment but then return to it; or, if the situation seems to warrant it, call a "facilitator's time out" and discuss what this step in the conversation calls for and why.

It won't always quell the resistance, but it is important that the "testing" participant—and everybody else in the group—understand that the purpose of the protocol is not to get everybody's questions answered, but to advance the learning of the presenter and the group as a whole in response to the questions and purposes for the protocol that everyone identified together.

Rejection

Rarely, a participant deliberately and, perhaps, persistently calls into question the value of using the protocol, or may explicitly question the authority of the facilitator or question her judgment in making a particular move. Faced with this level of resistance, the facilitator does not have the option of ignoring it (and hoping it will go away). At the same time, she needs to make sure that the "squeaky wheel" doesn't suck up so much of the facilitator's "oil" that the group is thrown off track.

Some of the same moves that help with participants who "test" can be helpful here: recognizing the objection but asking the participant to allow the conversation to continue as planned and to bring up the objection(s) when group gets to the debrief, or asking the group's permission to take a few minutes to discuss, as a group, the objection or question (however, this can eat up all the time the group has for the meeting). Other, more emphatic moves also might be needed: The facilitator might invite the objecting participant to act as a process observer rather than a participant, and to share his/her perspective on the process in the debrief step. Or, if the situation warrants, the facilitator might propose that the participant simply withdraw from the conversation.

While it may be of little help in the moment, the facilitator might suggest, after the protocol ends, that the resistant participant consider presenting some of his/her own students' work in a future protocol. This invitation can demonstrate a willingness on the facilitator's (and group's) part to offer the participant another way to experience and evaluate the process. Even if the resisting participant doesn't take the opportunity, he/she may have less of a case against the process.

*   *   *

Not all the challenges of facilitation are confined to facilitating protocols. Other challenges have to do with how groups come to a common purpose to begin with, how they decide on questions or problems to focus on, how they are put together (e.g., by grade level or across grades), as well as the ever-present question of how to find enough time, regularly enough, to carry out the work and allow it to deepen. While these challenges are beyond the scope of this book, facilitators should be involved in the decision-making process along with school administrators and others who seek to support collaborative inquiry into teaching and learning (see Weinbaum et al., 2004).

Chapter 9

How Do Facilitators Get Better?

Most facilitators we know draw on two sources for developing their skills: their own experiences as facilitators and their observations of other facilitators. In this brief chapter, we consider these and some other resources that can help facilitators improve their own practice. The strategies we identify below are usually practiced informally, sometimes even subconsciously, by facilitators. By making these strategies more visible, we hope to provide some tools for facilitators—at all levels of experience—to apply to their work.

OBSERVING AND EMULATING

If you think about how you learned any complex task, especially one that involves social interaction, such as dancing, speaking a new language, or teaching, you will quickly realize how much is learned through watching others do it and trying to follow their lead. When developing her own style and repertoire, a facilitator should take note of how other facilitators set the stage, tone, and pace for a group. As a teacher who often facilitates with the same partner said, "We learn from each other every time we work together."

Specific moves the facilitator observes other facilitators using may be integrated into, or adapted for, her own facilitation; however, trying too hard to sound or act like another facilitator can lead to wooden or awkward facilitation ("parroting"). The facilitator should be aware of her own style and what will work best and sound right coming from her (see Chapter 3). Sometimes a facilitator might publicly cite the source of a move she has adapted from another facilitator by saying something like, "In setting up this part of the protocol, a facilitator I've worked with sometimes says . . . ."

Finding opportunities to observe other facilitators can be challenging. It is certainly easier if other groups within the facilitator's school are using protocols, or if there are others in the facilitator's group who can rotate the facilitation role with her. An administrator or somebody from a partner organization (e.g., a school coach) may help identify opportunities for observation. Videotape can provide another resource for individual facilitators and groups to learn about facilitation. For example, in our facilitation workshops we have used a videotape of Gene Thompson-Grove facilitating a Tuning Protocol (see resources in Appendix A).

Observing others facilitate protocols for looking at student and teacher work is invaluable; however, facilitators can learn from observing other kinds of meetings, too—both in and out of school settings. It may be interesting to consider how the moves facilitators make in very different kinds of sessions, with different purposes, might be adapted for use in protocols.

In observing another facilitator at work, it is a good idea to record specific moves the facilitator makes. The "question pairs" below, drawn from the categories of moves outlined in Chapter 4, can guide observations and reflections about other facilitators (and, as discussed later in this chapter, about a facilitator's own facilitation):

- How does the facilitator get things started (setting the stage, setting the tone)? What are the observable consequences? (How does the group respond?)
- What does the facilitator do to help the group move through the protocol (setting the pace, encouraging depth, checking in with participants)? What are the consequences?
- What does the facilitator do to help the group debrief the protocol (inviting reflection, maintaining focus, supporting documentation)? What are the consequences?

EXPERIMENTING

The protocol is certainly a tremendous support for facilitation as a reference and guide. However, it is important to view the protocol-guided conversation not as a tightly scripted event, but rather as a place for experimentation and inquiry—compare it to a scientist's lab or artist's studio. Sometimes a facilitator may know in advance that she would like to try a particular move in a conversation; at other times, an occasion to try something new may emerge during the conversation. At times, it is possible (and appropriate) for a facilitator to inform the group that she is trying something different that may affect the conversation ("If it's okay with the group, I'd like to suggest we try . . . "); at other moments, the facilitator may choose to try a move that no one else may notice. Whenever possible, a facilitator should take note of how the group responds to the experiment—relying on memory is not always the best way to assess or access what happened at any specific point in the protocol. (See Chapter 7 on modifying and adapting protocols.)

ASKING FOR FEEDBACK

Reflecting on the process of the conversation is an essential component of most protocols. Typically, a "debriefing" stage is built into the protocol. During this stage, participants commonly offer comments on the facilitation as well as other features of the conversation (e.g., the structure of the protocol, the significance of the presenter's focusing question, and so on).

During the debriefing step, facilitators may choose to ask explicitly for feedback on the facilitation. Participants, however, might be reluctant to offer this feedback for fear of seeming critical of the facilitator. The facilitator might relieve this concern by asking for descriptive feedback on specific aspects of the facilitation (what was said and done) rather than (or prior to) asking for evaluative feedback ("the good, the bad, or the ugly"). The facilitator also might ask a colleague in the group or the school (or an outside partner familiar with the group's work) to observe the group and focus on facilitation. The observation question pairs above might be employed for this purpose.

REFLECTING

Despite the prominent role of reflection in most protocols, facilitators often find it easy to overlook the importance of reflecting on their work as facilitators. Many experienced facilitators attest to the benefit (as well as the difficulty!) of making time after a meeting, even if it is only a few minutes before the next class or on the drive or subway ride home, to reflect specifically on their own facilitation.

Finding time isn't the only challenge to productive self-reflection. Facilitators, like everybody else, can dwell on mistakes and missed opportunities, making reflection painful and less productive than a more balanced assessment would be. Using a brief protocol to guide reflection can ensure that the facilitator considers many aspects of the group's interactions and the conversation. Here are some possible steps to support reflection:

1. *Describe what happened, trying to refrain from judgment as much as possible. You might ask yourself questions such as*
   - What particular things did I or others say or do in the protocol that stand out in my mind? What responses did those words or actions seem to generate for myself or other group members?
   - During which parts of the protocol did people seem most engaged? Disengaged? Puzzled? Confident?
   - During which parts of the protocol did I feel most comfortable? What, if any, were the specific points that made me uncomfortable? What caused me to be uncomfortable? How did I respond?
   - What factors besides my facilitation seemed to have had an influence on the conversation?

2. *Identify strengths and weaknesses*
   - When did my facilitation seem to work well for the group? What makes me think so?
   - When did my efforts seem to fall flat? What makes me think so?
   - Do I feel that the facilitation was too little or too much? What were the moments when more/less/different facilitation might have been used?

3. *Name questions*
   - What questions do I have about my role and actions as a facilitator?

- What questions do I have about the group's conversation or the group members' interactions?

4. *Identify next steps*
   - How might I pursue my questions in order to develop some responses to them?
   - What things do I want to do differently for the next meeting?

Try to be specific and concrete as you review your role and the group's work.

DOCUMENTING

As discussed in Chapters 3 and 4, documentation is an important responsibility to which facilitators attend—and one of the most challenging. Facilitators benefit from finding or creating relatively "low-maintenance" ways to document their facilitation, as well as other important aspects of the group's work. For example, the facilitator might choose to use or adapt the observation questions above as a way to document her practice.

Some facilitators make time for reflective writing after a protocol or keep a journal that includes reflections on their facilitation, as well as notes about other aspects of the group's work. Such material provides a valuable springboard for examining and assessing both the facilitator's own work and the group's over time. If the facilitator or other group members keep such notes, they might periodically share and discuss them during the parts of the meeting devoted to reflection and planning next steps. In doing so, the facilitator can help the group build a collective picture of its learning.

*   *   *

For facilitators, as for basketball players, jazz musicians, and teachers, performance, practice, and improvement are inherently connected. Getting out onto the field or stage is a big step toward getting better at what they do. Observation, emulation, feedback, reflection, and documentation are some of the ways to get even more out of doing it.

Such strategies are important for improving one's facilitation work; but perhaps even more important is the mind-set or attitude that one cultivates through them. Facilitating protocols that nurture group learning is serious work—but work that is suffused throughout with a kind of play. Like a basketball game or a jazz performance, each protocol-guided conversation is a unique and unpredictable event. A facilitator, like the point guard of the basketball team or the leader of the jazz band, is a catalyst for the group's work but can never completely control the outcome.

Each meeting offers the possibility of new learning as well as new stumbling blocks. Sometimes a key basket is scored, sometimes a critical pass is stolen. Sometimes the jazz solo soars; sometimes it wanders. Sometimes, in a learning conversation, new insights flourish; and sometimes the conversation feels flat.

The successes are not random: They evolve from the twin commitments to work (discipline, patient practice, regular skill building) and play (seeking new opportunities, taking risks, cultivating curiosity). For facilitators of protocols, then, disciplined reflection, thorough preparation, and skill development by themselves are not sufficient. Equally important are a sense of adventure—indeed, a sense of humor!—and a willingness to embrace ambiguity and uncertainty. Conversations will not go as expected. The answers to complex questions of teaching and learning are never readily apparent. As Rilke says, "We must learn to love the questions themselves."

Taking questions seriously—and helping group members to do the same—is the essence of the facilitator's work. Questions that arise from personal experience and reflection, that are cultivated and honed in collaboration with colleagues, that are pursued through rigorous as well as playful exploration, will take both facilitators and the groups they work with where they need to go. In protocols, as in most other professional and personal endeavors, it is the questions, after all, that make real learning possible.

Appendix A:
Additional Resources

Appendix B:
Activities

References

About the Authors

Additional Resources

In addition to the books listed in the References section, several other resources contain useful information for facilitators of protocols.

WEBSITES

Looking at Student Work (LASW): www.lasw.org

This resource was developed by the national Looking at Student Work Collaborative and is maintained by the National School Reform Faculty at the Harmony School and Education Center. It contains protocols, resources for using and facilitating protocols, and references to research on looking at student work.

National School Reform Faculty (NSRF): www.nsrfharmony.org

The website of the National School Reform Faculty provides information about NSRF centers of activity around the country and opportunities for professional development, including NSRF institutes and Critical Friends Group coaches' trainings. It also includes resources, including a comprehensive set of protocols, activities, and readings that support looking at student and teacher work collaboratively, building professional learning communities, engaging in collaborative inquiry, and becoming a facilitative leader.

National School Reform Faculty New York Center:
www.nsrfnewyork.org

The website of the National School Reform Faculty's New York Center contains a comprehensive set of protocols (and facilitator tips) for looking at student and teacher work, teaching and coaching dilemmas, and so on.

VIDEOS

Looking at Student Work: A Window into the Classroom.
Annenberg Institute for School Reform/Teachers College Press
(www.aisr.org; www.tcpress.edu)

> This video provides an overview of looking at student work as a
> strategy for school reform. It features teachers and administrators at
> Norview High School in Norfolk, Virginia—a member of the
> ATLAS Communities school redesign program—taking part in a
> protocol for looking at student work, and discussing with other
> teachers, administrators, and staff developers their experiences with
> looking at student work .

*Reflecting on Teaching Practice: Student Work, Teacher Work, and
Standards (Part I—Math).* Annenberg/CPB: Critical Issues in
School Reform (www.learner.org)

> In this video, a tenth-grade math teacher from San Bruno,
> California, presents a sample of student work from her classroom to
> a group of educators. The group uses the Tuning Protocol (facilitat-
> ed by Gene Thompson-Grove) to examine this work, give the
> teacher feedback, and discuss its implications for her teaching prac-
> tice. This video is a useful teaching tool for groups and individuals
> learning about protocols and facilitation.

Activities

The two activities presented here serve as resources for learning about facilitation through practice in simulated protocols or pre-protocol settings. Both are written for groups but also may be used by individuals as further illustration of ideas discussed earlier in the book (i.e., challenging situations facilitators sometimes must deal with or conferencing with the presenting teacher in preparation for a protocol).

The first activity provides a collection of scenarios that, although fictitious, attempt to capture some of the real-life challenges facilitators encounter. The activity asks for the group to "read" each situation and consider which "moves" might be employed to resolve it productively for the entire group. The second activity is focused on an important aspect of protocol preparation treated in Chapter 7: matching the purpose for using a protocol and the presenter's interest or question with the most appropriate protocol.

ACTIVITY I: FACILITATION SCENARIOS

The scenarios provided below illustrate some key moments in fictional, but plausible, protocols. We offer them here as an opportunity for readers to reflect on facilitation challenges in a more contextualized way. Of course, just as in actual protocols, none of the scenarios below has a single right response. We hope these scenarios will serve as a departure point for considering a range of productive moves that a facilitator might make in a given situation, as well as the possible consequences of those moves.

This activity will be most useful to readers after they have reviewed Chapters 3, 4, and 8. The steps below describe a process for using the scenarios as the starting point for group discussion about facilitation.

If the group is large, we suggest dividing into smaller groups of four to six.

Steps in the Activity

1. Choose a facilitator for the discussion of the first scenario.
2. Everybody reads the scenario silently. (The facilitator also may read the scenario aloud.)
3. The facilitator asks participants to put the problem(s) embedded in the scenario into their own words: "How do you read the situation? What might be the underlying issues or problems?" [*Note*: This third step is important. The group may want to dive immediately into deciding what the facilitator should do; however, resisting that temptation long enough to first discuss the problems will yield a richer conversation in the following step.]
4. When the group has reached a shared understanding of the problem(s), the facilitator asks, "How would you, as the facilitator, respond? What are some moves you might make? What are the likely consequences of each?" [*Note*: Often, at this point in the exercise, group members may be inclined to discuss all the things the facilitator in the scenario should have done *before* the protocol began in order to prevent the problem altogether. While generating these ideas can be useful, the group also should give real attention to the actual moment described in the scenario and how to deal with it. In real protocols, even when the facilitator is experienced and the presenting teacher and the participants are well prepared, things can veer away from the plan in mid-protocol. The point of these scenarios is to give everyone a chance to work on developing the insights and skills that are essential to addressing such situations in the moments when they arise.]
5. Through discussion, the group may or may not come to agreement about a promising response (or several). The point is not to reach consensus but to seek out and consider different interpretations of the problem(s) found in the scenarios, as well as a range of moves that might be employed to address the problem(s) and their likely outcomes.

6. The group may choose to go on to another scenario (and take turns facilitating).

Scenario 1

In your third meeting as a group, you are feeling pretty good about the way things are going. Today, for example, Kurt is presenting some samples from his sixth graders' math portfolios. In the feedback discussion, the group seems eager to talk about the kinds of strategies students are using. In the first few protocols the group had gone through in previous meetings, most people appeared to be quite comfortable joining the conversation to make a comment or ask a question. Increasingly, the discussion in the protocols has felt like a more natural conversation, with people building on one another's comments, sometimes asking one another questions. In fact, lately you have been finding it a bit challenging to break in to ask a question or suggest moving to the next step of the protocol.

As you look around the table, you notice that Maria, a fourth-grade bilingual teacher, has not said anything during this protocol. She seems engaged, looking at the work samples and listening to others' comments and questions. In thinking back on the previous protocols the group has done, you can't think of a specific instance in which she did speak, although you have a vague memory that she asked a clarifying question in the first protocol the group went through (the one people dubbed the "training wheels protocol" because everybody was so careful to follow the steps on the paper). As the feedback discussion continues, you find yourself losing track of the movement of the discussion. It will soon be time to move to the presenter's response to the feedback. How do you read this situation? What, if anything, should you do?

Scenario 2

In a Tuning Protocol, Jim is presenting a community service project his middle school students carried out with a local day care center. In the project, his students interviewed the children about their interests, heroes, and so on. Then, back in their own classroom, Jim's students wrote and illustrated books featuring the children they interviewed. Jim begins his presentation with an impassioned description of his students and the challenges he has faced in working with them. "This has been a real breakthrough in working with this group," he explains enthusiastically. He begins to tell an anecdote about one of his "toughest cases" sitting down with a little boy at the day care center. Glancing at your watch, you realize almost half the time for his presentation is already over, and he hasn't yet talked about the goals for the project, the assessment plan, or the student work; nor has he given his focusing question. You look around the table and see that the participants seem very interested in his story, but time is marching on . . .

Scenario 3

During the warm and cool feedback segment of a protocol (a step during which the presenter is not permitted to respond), Lena, a respected senior colleague in the group, begins to list the weaknesses, as she sees them, of the student work and the assignment. Lena is not negative in her tone and, in fact, frames her comments constructively, saying things like, "It will help a lot if you don't . . . ." The other participants listen attentively, although, as Lena goes on, some begin to shift in their seats. The presenter herself is avidly taking notes on everything Lena says. As the "dos" and "don'ts" add up, you wonder whether to intervene and, if so, how . . .

Scenario 4

The Consultancy you are facilitating has reached the step in which the participants ask the presenter clarifying questions. Jeanie, a fourth-grade teacher, has presented a dilemma about preparing students for the state math and writing tests in spring (it's December) and continuing the project-based curriculum she has been developing with other fourth-grade teachers for the past 3 years. One participant immediately asks, "How will the standardized tests and the mandated changes in curriculum affect the narrative report cards we've just implemented here at the school?" You suggest that might not be a strictly clarifying question. "Good," Jeanie says, "because I have *no* idea." The next couple of questions ("How much time do the kids have each day to work on projects?" and "Can you give a quick example of a project you have done with your class?") are more typical clarifying questions. But then the questions again tilt toward addressing bigger issues of curriculum and assessment as they connect to the state testing—something that is clearly on everybody's mind. You are feeling like the protocol is sliding away from Jeanie's specific concerns into something larger the group really wants (even needs) to discuss. What is going on here, and what do you do?

Scenario 5

The warm and cool feedback portion of the protocol has been good and substantive. You are looking forward to hearing Laura, the presenting teacher, talk about some of the things that came up. She's eager to start off, and thanks the group sincerely for their comments. Then she says, "Let me just explain a few things that I didn't say before about my class and the assignment." She seems to be going through all the feedback points she recorded and providing more background details for each. She keeps going, not exactly defending her work or the students', but not really addressing the feedback that came up either. What can you do to help Laura take advantage of the feedback as a chance to genuinely reflect on (rather than explain or defend) her practice?

Scenario 6

Craig has presented an inquiry project that involves students working in teams to solve a "mystery story" he has written. In order to solve the mystery, which has to do with water levels in the local pond, students must complete a series of mathematical calculations, mostly having to do with volume. Craig has shared the work samples from two student groups. He rated one group's work "distinguished" and the other "proficient." During the period for examining student work, you realize that both samples contain a raft of errors in calculation. Craig's rubric includes "make accurate calculations" as one of its main points. As the participants' feedback begins, it seems clear to you that they are concentrating on the cleverness of the assignment and the positive interactions within the student groups and, intentionally or not, staying away from how Craig scored these groups. Do you step in? How?

Scenario 7

Your group is using a protocol that includes a step for asking clarifying questions. When you invite the group to ask clarifying questions, Dwight says, "I really like the way this assignment is set up. I did a similar thing with my class last year, and the results were great!" He goes on to describe a bit about the work his students did. When he pauses, you take the opportunity to gently remind the group that this is really a time simply to ask clarifying questions and that the time for deeper discussion happens a few steps later. Dwight sighs, rolls his eyes, and says, disparagingly, "Whatever. I'm not really sure why we need a 'protocol' anyway." No one says anything, and you are not sure whether to let this comment go or deal with it now . . .

Scenario 8

As part of the superintendent's professional development day, you have been asked to facilitate a protocol for looking at student work for a group of district administrators who have expressed interest in this approach to professional development. You've asked Carolee, an eighth-grade teacher from the teacher inquiry group you regularly facilitate, to present. She selects a sample of student writing from a boy in her class whose work she finds very creative in some ways, although quite limited in others. The group is looking at the work using the Collaborative Assessment Conference, so Carolee passes out the writing sample, a one-page story called "In the City," without giving the group any context about the assignment or the student. After the group spends a few minutes looking at the work, you invite participants to share their descriptions of the piece. "In the Collaborative Assessment Conference," you tell them, "we begin by trying to describe what we see in the piece, as concretely as possible, and stay away from making interpretations of the work or judgments about it." A principal you don't know well raises his hand, and you call on him. "Well, I'm not sure if this is what you're looking for, but I'd use the word 'primitive' to describe this." Silence in the group. At this point, what might you do?

Scenario 9

You are facilitating a Tuning Protocol for a high school group new to using protocols. Alex presents a project in which students applied math skills to solve real-world problems of height and volume, then presented their solutions and explained their process. Alex shares her focusing question with the group: "How can I help the students do better work on this assignment?" The presentation goes well, you think; however, you are concerned that during the period for looking at the student work, only a few participants seemed actually to be looking at the student work closely. As soon as you invite warm and cool feedback, one of the participants volunteers, "I just think it's wonderful to see students engaged in real-world problems. I'd love to see this happening more in my school." As other participants join the discussion, you grow more and more uncomfortable with the feedback: It's all quite warm, and Alex seems to be enjoying hearing it. (She writes a few things down at the beginning and then just listens.) However, none of the comments relate very directly to the student work samples she has shared. The clock is ticking . . . What do you do?

Scenario 10

Barry has volunteered to present at the group's next meeting. In the few protocols the group has done so far, Barry has proven a bit of a challenge to facilitate. He is a very enthusiastic participant with lots to say, but tends to lose track of (or to disregard) what the protocol calls for at any given point. You also have noticed that most of what Barry says tends to come back to his own story or ideas. For example, in one recent protocol, during the period for questioning the presenter, Barry launched into a story about one of the "wild" projects he did with his students in his previous school. In another protocol, during the period for offering feedback, he gave a mini-treatise on his own educational philosophy. As one of the other participants put it in a private conversation after the last protocol: "Barry's great. I'd love to go have a beer with him sometime, but he's 'out there.'"

You set up a preconference with Barry to talk about his presentation for the next meeting. He tells you he'll have no problem picking out samples of student work to present. He starts to talk about one possibility, a project his students currently are working on, but before he can describe its goals or what stage the students are at with it, he jumps to an idea he has for a new course he'd like to develop on political theory. When you say you need to get to your next class soon and it would be good to have an idea of what Barry will present, he says, "Don't worry,

I have a couple of ideas I think the group is going to love." What are the issues here? How might you respond to Barry? What are some practical steps you can take to help Barry prepare and ensure that the protocol discussion will be a productive learning experience for the whole group?

ACTIVITY II: PROTOCOL MATCHING

This activity is adapted from one developed by Gene Thompson-Grove, Simone Waite, and Faith Dunne of the National School Reform Faculty. It is designed to help you match a protocol to a particular teacher's concerns and the work that s/he wants to share.

As in the scenarios in Activity I, there is no single right answer to any of the scenarios presented below. Arguments can be made to use different protocols for the same piece of work, depending on the teacher's particular need or concern. However, there are protocols that clearly don't fit a particular scenario. Eliminate those protocols first, then choose what might be appropriate for the work and the question the teacher has.

The scenarios below can be addressed with the three protocols that are included in Chapter 1:

- the Collaborative Assessment Conference
- the Consultancy
- the Tuning Protocol

To do this activity, it will be necessary to have these protocols easily accessible, as well as the chart that summarizes them in Chapter 7 (Figure 7.1). Of course, dozens of other protocols exist, any one of which might (or might not) be appropriate for any of the situations below. (See *The Power of Protocols* by McDonald et al., 2003.)

Steps in the Activity

1. Scan the protocols in Figures 1.2–1.4 or in Figure 7.1.
2. Read the scenarios and jot down your first thoughts about which protocols might be useful to the teacher and which

ones clearly are not. (Writing on sticky notes may make it easier to compare notes with other participants in the next step.)

3. Move into groups of three or four and compare notes. Go through one scenario at a time, taking notes on your points of agreement and difference. Go back to the protocols the group chose and re-read them carefully.
4. Talk again about which one or two protocols might work, and how you would go about picking one. Remember, in the protocol, you don't have to look at all of the work the teacher has.
5. Note what questions you might need to ask the presenter to be sure that this is the best choice of protocol.

Scenario 1

By March, Karla, who teaches elementary school, doesn't know what to do about Hannah, a second grader whom she also had as a first grader. Hannah has some language-related problems, including a speech articulation difficulty. Her writing is not close to being at grade level, yet informal reading assessments suggest that she is reading above grade level. Getting Hannah to write even a few sentences is like pulling teeth. Karla has exhausted her repertoire with Hannah and wants some guidance on what to do next. She has brought several pieces of Hannah's written work and some comparative pieces from other students in the class. She is willing to work with any or all of the student work she has brought to answer her question about how to help Hannah improve her writing skills.

Scenario 2

Bruce teaches eighth-grade science. He has developed an earth science curriculum that focuses on inquiry projects, labs, and cooperative learning. This year he has in his class three students who have behavior problems ranging from inappropriate interpersonal behavior to some more severe behavior disorders. These students have an aide assigned to them full-time, but she can't manage adequately unless the class is doing very structured work—teacher-led questions and answers, or silent work at their desks. When small groups are working collaboratively, or when individuals are moving around the room to work on labs or projects, these three students often become vocally disruptive. Bruce does not want to dismantle a curriculum that serves the rest of the class well, but he doesn't know what to do. He has brought several pieces of these students' work and also a couple of projects that small groups have done, which he believes demonstrate the success of his curriculum.

Scenario 3

Monica is a high school special education teacher. She co-teaches with a ninth-grade English teacher. They recently tried an alternative assessment with their third-period class (a mix of regular and special education students) in which they had the students create story maps about *The Diary of Anne Frank*. She has three examples from the class that represent the level of work the students completed. She thinks students did a "decent job" but wonders if most students "dug deeply enough" into the text. She would like to use this type of alternative assessment in the future (all the kids enjoyed it and all, including the special education students, actually were talking about the text), but she needs some guidance and wants to hear others' perspectives.

Scenario 4

Jamal is a high school art teacher. This is his second year as a teacher. He has a student, Mike, in his class who baffles him. Mike takes each assignment and does something with it that is different from everyone else's work. If the others are working on form, he seems to be experimenting with color. If they are doing still life, he seems to be working on abstraction (although he can do representational drawing when he wants to). He also refuses to write in the journal Jamal asks students to keep as homework while they are working on each art project. "I don't need to write," he says. "This is an art class." Jamal isn't sure what to make of Mike's work, since it is so different from everyone else's. He has brought a sample of Mike's work and several comparative samples from the same assignment done by other students.

Scenario 5

Ted is a science educational specialist in a large school district. He is responsible for all of the secondary schools, including the alternative high school. He began his tenure by working with a majority of the secondary science teachers in innovative teaching strategies that encourage critical thinking. Teachers in four of the six schools have been using the new strategies, many with great success, but most of the teachers in the remaining two schools are still working in a "business as usual" mode. He would like to find a way to encourage the teachers in these two schools to at least try some of the strategies before he has to report on his work to the district's K–12 science curriculum coordinator. Ted is eager to hear any and all suggestions.

Scenario 6

Ronald is a fourth-grade teacher. He has a math assignment he has given for the past several years that asks students to demonstrate what they know about elementary geometry (shapes, lines, and angles) by creating advertisements for innovative products. His students from past years have loved the assignment and he has given virtually the same assignment for the past 3 years with good success. Students have looked forward to the assignment and have come to fourth grade knowing they would "get to do it." This year, however, he was dismayed by the lack of interest and effort by students, and by the lack of creativity in the final products. Students did the work, but essentially either used his examples or used ideas from students' work in past years, and did little else that was new. He is wondering if it is time to create a fresh, new assignment, or if he simply needs to make changes in the current assignment. He has the assignment, a "pretty rudimentary" rubric he used for the first time this year in assessing the work, a range of samples from this year's class, and a couple of outstanding examples from past years that he showed the class before they began.

References

The references for this book include a number of excellent resources for facilitators and other participants in groups that use protocols to look at student and teacher work. The following codes indicate areas of particular focus:

- Collaborative inquiry (CI)
- Facilitation (F)
- Protocols (P)

Allen, D. (Ed.). (1998). *Assessing student learning: From grading to understanding*. New York: Teachers College Press. (CI, F, P)

Ball, D. L., & Cohen, D. K. (1999). Developing practice, developing practitioners: Toward a practice-based theory of professional education. In L. Darling-Hammond & G. Sykes (Eds.), *Teaching as the learning profession: Handbook of policy and practice* (pp. 3–32). San Francisco: Jossey-Bass. (CI)

Blythe, T., Allen, D., & Powell, B. S. (1999). *Looking together at student work: A companion guide to assessing student learning*. New York: Teachers College Press. (F, P)

Bray, J. N., Smith, L. L., Lee, J., & Yorks, L. (2000). *Collaborative inquiry in practice: Action, reflection, and meaning making*. Thousand Oaks, CA: Sage. (CI, F)

Cazden, C. (2001). *Classroom discourse: The language of teaching and learning* (2nd ed.). Portsmouth, NH: Heinemann.

Clark, C. M. (2001). Good conversation. In C. M. Clark (Ed.), *Talking shop: Authentic conversation and teacher learning* (pp. 172–182). New York: Teachers College Press. (CI)

Cuban, L. (2001). *How can I fix it? Finding solutions and managing dilemmas: An educator's road map*. New York: Teachers College Press.

Evidence Project Staff. (2001). *The evidence process: A collaborative approach to understanding and improving teaching and learning.* Cambridge, MA: Harvard Project Zero. (CI, F, P)

Himley, M., with Carini, P. F. (2000). *From another angle: Children's strengths and school standards.* New York: Teachers College Press. (CI, P)

Killion, J. P., & Simmons, L. A. (1992). The Zen of facilitation. *Journal of Staff Development, 13*(3), 2–5. (F)

Lieberman, A., & Miller, L. (2000). Teaching and teacher development: A new synthesis for a new century. In R. S. Brandt (Ed.), *Education in a new era: Association for Supervision and Curriculum Development yearbook 2000* (pp. 47–66). Alexandria, VA: Association for Supervision and Curriculum Development.

Little, J. W., Gearhart, M., Curry, M., & Kafka, J. (2003). Looking at student work for teacher learning, teacher community, and school reform. *Phi Delta Kappan, 85*(3), 184–192. (CI)

Louis, K. S., Kruse, S. D., & Marks, H. M. (1996). Schoolwide professional community. In F. M. Newmann & Associates (Eds.), *Authentic achievement: Restructuring schools for intellectual quality* (pp. 179–203). San Francisco: Jossey-Bass. (CI)

McDonald, J., Mohr, N., Dichter, A., & McDonald, E. (2003). *The power of protocols: An educator's guide to better practice.* New York: Teachers College Press. (P)

Moffett, J. A. (2000). Sustaining change: The answers are blowing in the wind. *Educational Leadership, 57*(7), 35–38.

Newmann, F. M., Lopez, G., & Bryk, A. S. (1998, October). *The quality of intellectual work in Chicago schools: A baseline report.* Chicago: Consortium of Chicago School Research.

Sarason, S. (1999). *Teaching as a performing art.* New York: Teachers College Press.

Tishman, S., Perkins, D. N., & Jay, E. (1995). *The thinking classroom: Learning and teaching in a culture of thinking.* Needham, MA: Allyn & Bacon.

Tripp, D. (1993). *Critical incidents in teaching: Developing professional judgement.* London: Routledge.

Weinbaum, A., Allen, D., Blythe, T., Simon, K., Seidel, S., & Rubin, C. (2004). *Teaching as Inquiry: Asking Hard Questions to Improve Practice and Student Achievement.* New York: Teachers College Press. (CI, F)

About the Authors

David Allen is a researcher at the National Center for Restructuring Education, Schools, and Teaching (NCREST), Teachers College, Columbia University. He has worked at Project Zero, Harvard Graduate School of Education, and the Coalition of Essential Schools, Brown University, on projects related to collaborative teacher inquiry, looking at student work, and authentic assessment. He is the editor of *Assessing Student Learning: From Grading to Understanding* (Teachers College Press, 1998), co-author (with Tina Blythe and Barbara S. Powell) of *Looking Together at Student Work* (Teachers College Press, 1999), and a co-author of *Teaching as Inquiry: Asking Hard Questions to Improve Practice and Student Achievement* (Teachers College Press, 2004). He has taught English and ESL at middle school, high school, and college levels. In 1996, he received a Fulbright research grant to study school reform in Poland.

Tina Blythe has been a researcher with Project Zero, Harvard Graduate School of Education, since 1988. She has focused on professional development, teacher inquiry, and collaborative assessment of student work, as well as on curriculum and instruction that emphasize learning for understanding in classrooms and after-school programs. She has taught middle school, high school, and university courses. She currently teaches in the faculty development program of the Boston Architectural Center. She is the principal author of *The Teaching for Understanding Guide* (Jossey-Bass, 1998) and co-author (with David Allen and Barbara S. Powell) of *Looking Together at Student Work* (Teachers College Press, 1999). She has collaborated on a number of other books and articles, including *Fun Learning Matters: Doing Projects in Afterschool Programs* (The After-School Corporation, 2001), and *Teaching as Inquiry: Asking Hard Questions to Improve Practice and Student Achievement* (Teachers College Press, 2004).

Gene Thompson-Grove has been Co-Director of the National School Reform Faculty (NSRF), a national program begun at the Annenberg Institute for School Reform and now housed at the Harmony Education Center in Bloomington, Indiana, from 1995 to the present. NSRF works with educators to create and sustain professional learning communities in their schools through Critical Friends Groups (CFG) and other programs. Through NSRF, she coordinates the national Looking at Student Work Collaborative. She is also one of the developers of the Looking at Student Work website (*www.lasw.org*), is the author of the Consultancy protocol, and has written various other protocols and support materials for studying student work collaboratively. In addition to her work with NSRF, Thompson-Grove works with several reform organizations and school districts, and facilitates national and regional seminars on examining student work collaboratively, understanding school culture, creating professional communities in schools, and engaging in collaborative inquiry.